S

IN THE ALPS

OTHER SELF-CATERING GUIDES PUBLISHED BY CHRISTOPHER HELM

Self-catering Afloat
Bill Glenton

Self-catering in France
Arthur and Barbara Eperon

Self-catering in Greece, Mainland and Islands
Florica Kyriacopoulos and Tim Salmon

Self-catering in Italy
Susan Grossman

Self-catering in Portugal
Carol Wright

Self-catering in Spain
Carole Stewart with Chris Stewart

SELF-CATERING IN THE ALPS

Anne Williams

CHRISTOPHER HELM
London

Line illustrations by Mike Dodd and Lorna Turpin
Christopher Helm (Publishers) Ltd, Imperial House,
21-25 North Street, Bromley, Kent BR1 1SD

ISBN 0-7470-3405-2

A CIP catalogue record for this book
is available from the British Library

Printed and bound in Great Britain
by Billing and Sons, Worcester.

Contents

Acknowledgements

I would like to thank the following people and organisations for their considerable help in the detailed research for this book:

Janet Chisholm of Ski PR for arranging my travel; ex-chalet cooks Elaine Ngan and Debbie Burridge; ski journalist Steve Pooley; and Caroline Magnus for help with the German phrases. Also, The French Government Tourist Office, Food and Wine from France, The Swiss Centre, Nestlé in Switzerland, Cheeses from Switzerland, the Aosta Valley Tourist Board, The Italian Trade Centre, Enoteca Wine Centre, The Austrian National Tourist Office and The Austrian Trade Commission.

1

Introduction

This guide is aimed at the thousands of skiers who have chosen to book a self-catering apartment instead of joining a chalet party or staying in a hotel with full board. Saving money is just one reason for this decision; a desire for more freedom to keep your own hours and meal times is another. The information and recipes are intended to be as informative and practical as possible, bearing in mind that you are there to enjoy the skiing, not to spend hours in the kitchen.

WHY SELF-CATERING?

The ski resorts of the Alps are fast becoming some of Britain's most popular holiday destinations. What used to be an exclusive holiday for the few, due to the expense and time involved in travelling to small Alpine villages several hundred metres up, has now become (thanks to the tour operators) something we can all enjoy for as little as a week or even a weekend, with the minimum of fuss.

None the less, despite the ease with which you can now reach your resort, and the network of lifts which whisk you to the top of the slopes in six easy minutes instead of several hours of laborious climbing on skis, the price must still be paid for all this comfort and organisation. When booking a winter sports holiday, you not only have to bear in mind the travel cost (usually by air) and your accommodation, if you don't possess your own gear, which is an expensive capital outlay, you must hire protective clothing, skis, boots, poles — and, on top of that, buy a lift pass which itself can be anything from £30 to £100 for one week. Ski school instruction may be needed, and you will want to buy ski goggles or good sunglasses as well as proper gloves for safety as well as comfort.

All in all it is an expensive business and one reason why increasing numbers of people are turning to self-catering accommodation as a good way of keeping the cost down. Your own flat, rented for the duration, is not only much cheaper, but also provides a more informal, private and flexible base for a small group of friends, and in particular for a family with children.

However tolerant some of our Continental neighbours may be of small children, no parent enjoys coping with a five-year-old's tantrum in the middle of a hotel dining room. Even older children can prove difficult when it comes to eating unfamiliar dishes in strange surroundings, and any age gets bored sitting listening to adults discuss the different technical merits of their new skis over a lengthy meal. Cooking food in your own self-catering apartment, if not for yourself at least for the children's evening meal, provides the ideal answer.

CUTTING DOWN ON THE WORK

Nobody goes on a self-catering skiing holiday in order to spend it in the kitchen. Skiing is an absorbing, exhilarating, time-consuming and fairly exhausting sport. It will take up most of your day, whether you're the type who likes spending hours off-piste in virgin snow, or whether as an intermediate you are determined to try that run just one more time. Even beginners, who may not want to ski all day, will find their aching muscles just want to collapse into an armchair or a bar at the end of the day.

Food is therefore not a principal part of your holiday, as it can be on more leisurely trips around the Mediterranean, when happy hours are to be spent wandering around local markets or lingering over long lunches on the terrace of your villa. However, it does play an important role and should be given a certain amount of thought and attention, both as a vital fuel to give you the energy to tackle the slopes, and as a focus for your après-ski life, which is all part of an enjoyable holiday in the Alps.

Bitter experience has taught me that a skimpy breakfast can lead to a mid-morning energy crisis. If you are unfit this can be quite severe, making you feel faint, dizzy or even sick as you try to push your body to limits it is unused to, with no reserves to fall back on. A good lunch on the slopes likewise is important to recharge the batteries if you are to continue skiing throughout the afternoon, as well as being an excuse for the less fit to ease off their ski boots and have a good rest! By evening everyone is looking forward to a hot shower (or bath if you are lucky) and a big informal meal, generally accompanied by liberal quantities of beer or wine.

Most of the recipes here are built around the limited time, enthusiasm and equipment you will have to devote to cooking. They are interesting and yet easy to prepare, use a sensible balance of convenience food and fresh local ingredients, and provide filling and tasty meals with the minimum of fuss.

RECIPES

I have divided the book country by country. For each one you will find a full guide to what you can expect to find in the local shops as well as regional specialities to look out for. There is also information on local wines and other drinks, and a section which describes typical local dishes as well as giving recipes for some of them. Many of these take a little longer and cost a bit extra to make yourself and you will probably want to wait till you get home to try them out. Some, however, are ideal for a party or last night celebration, particularly since the required ingredients will be right at hand.

There are also recipes for easy everyday meals to cook while you are at the resort that are quick and simple (many apartment kitchens have no oven and only two rings). These are divided into suggestions for packed lunches and delicious fillings for sandwiches, and recipes for soups and starters, everyday supper dishes and salads.

Precise quantities are not essential and, bearing in mind that you will not have access to scales and measuring jugs, I have given either an appropriate packet, tin or carton size or an easy 'round' quantity of fresh ingredients. You will be buying everything in metric weights and volumes, but I have given rough imperial equivalents in brackets for those of us who still find it difficult to 'think metric'.

All spoon measurements are rounded (i.e. as much above as below). A useful liquid measure is a standard coffee mug, which holds ½ pint (300ml) or you could use a small 150ml or 150g tub of cream, yoghurt or cream cheese which holds about ¼ pint. For measuring larger amounts of liquid for soups and casseroles, remember that a bottle of wine holds 1¾ pints (¾ litre).

DRINKS

As explained above, the local wines and spirits are detailed under each country. It is always fun to throw a party on holiday, and so I have included a few cocktail recipes to help you forget your aching muscles and indulge in some après-ski.

SHOPPING

Shops in ski resorts, since they have a captive market, inevitably charge higher prices, sometimes substantially higher — particularly the supermarkets geared specifically towards the self-catering skier. If you have someone in your party who is not such a keen skier and decides to take a day trip down the valley to the nearest town, make sure they bring back a good selection of the more expensive items (although it would be unfair to ask them to carry around bagfuls of heavy, bulky food and drink). Or if you are travelling out by car, stop at the closest decent-sized town to your resort and stock up on food and drink before you get there.

Bear in mind always that local brands and specialities are bound to cost less than those you are used to at home, so try and wean your children off expensive breakfast cereals or marmalade before they leave Britain. All supermarkets stock essentials like soap powder, washing up liquid, etc., although usually in irritatingly large sizes — if you're going for just a week it may be worth taking a small jar or packet of your own to save money.

Although resorts which are based around an old village will probably have some kind of small supermarket, there is likely to be a clutch of older specialist shops as well: the butcher and poultry shop, baker, cheesemonger, greengrocer and so on. Do use these places as well as the supermarket; you're much more likely to find the local specialities in them and it's a chance to meet the locals too.

LANGUAGE

Lastly, I have included an easy reference section on how to shop in another language. The words for the different food-stuffs have already been given in the country by country guide, and choosing your produce is less problematic anyway, since you can always point! But asking if the butcher has something cheaper, or whether the greengrocer can supply you with a carrier bag, is less easy to mime and often requires a few phrases in the language, however badly pronounced!

FRANCE

2

SHOPPING IN THE FRENCH ALPS

World famous for its cooking, France is also one of the best places in Europe to shop for food. Each region has its specialities, evolved from the different type of soil, landscape and economic structure of that area. Ski resorts in the French Alps are highly sophisticated when it comes to shopping, and you will find, particularly in the purpose-built ones in Savoie, every type of food imaginable, including pre-cooked and even, in some places, takeaway hot dishes. Further south in Dauphiné the older resorts, frequented more by French independent skiers than the British tour operators, continue much as they have always done with village shops and a new supermarket.

In both areas, it is always worth selecting the regional foods when you see them. You will also find that specialities of the Rhône valley to the west and Provence to the south have crept up the mountains onto the shelves. Outlined below are just a few of the things to look out for in particular.

DELICATESSEN

Whether you are shopping in the supermarket in a purpose-built resort, or the little shops in the older villages, you will find a good range of delicatessen goods. These have always been a bonus of shopping in France, and help you cut down on the cooking considerably (although at a price of course).

In traditional villages you may find a separate *charcuterie*, a *traiteur* (which sells ready-to-eat dishes) and an *épicerie* (grocer), or they may be combined into one. Many of the goods sold can be also found at the staffed delicatessen counter in a good supermarket. The French style 'take away' food is a boon on a self-catering holiday. You will find salads, savoury and sweet flans, pies, and ready-cooked dishes for re-heating. These are not cheap, but certainly convenient.

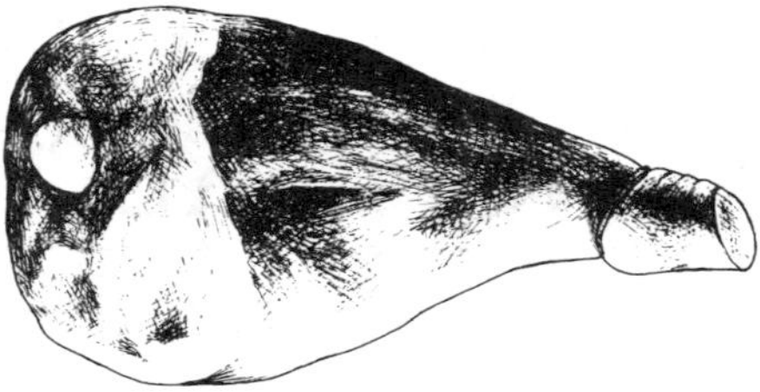

Smoked ham

There is a lot of *charcuterie* made in the French Alps and you should definitely try the local varieties. Apart from the usual *saucisses* and *rosettes* you will find delicious and unusual smoked hams from Celliers and Taninges in Savoie, or one called Luxeuil. Look out for *saucisses au cumin* flavoured with anis from the nearby Jura and herby sausages from Annecy called *pormonniers*, which must be cooked before eating. Dauphiné offers a cumin and caraway flavoured sausage called *murcon*, a boiling variety called *sabadon*, little pork faggots (*caillettes*) and *diots*, which are made of pork and vegetables and preserved in wine — cook these before eating.

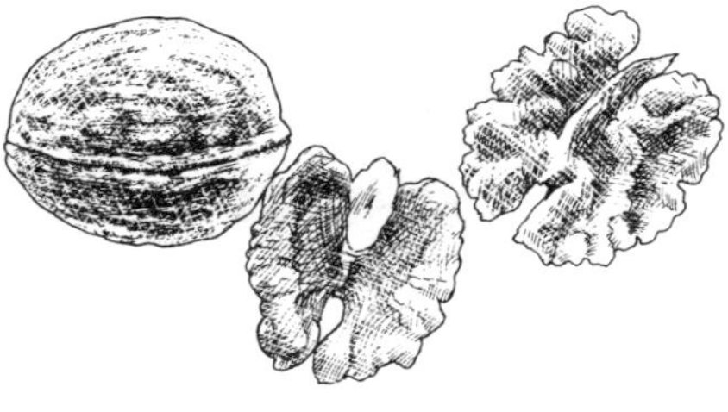

Walnuts

Walnut oil (*huile de noix*) is made in great quantity around Grenoble (much of it sent for export) and is a good bargain to take home. White truffles are a speciality in Savoie, the season unfortunately ending just as the skiing starts, but you may still find them on sale in cans.

As in all French delicatessens, you will find a good range of tinned vegetables like peas (*petits pois*), ratatouille, pimentos, artichoke hearts (*coeurs d'artichaut*) and all the little delicacies that make a salad something special. Tea (*thé*) and coffee (*café*) are expensive and may be worth taking with you, but olive oil (*huile d'olive*) as well as the walnut variety is a good buy.

Cheeses (*Fromages*)

These are sold in delicatessens and supermarkets. The French Alps are a major centre for dairy products and there are dozens of different types of cheese used in cooking and for eating before the dessert or for snacks.

Beaufort This is the king of the creamy *gruyère* cheeses, made in small amounts by independent producers. It comes in big rounds weighing 40–50kg (88–110lb) with a reddish-brown, smooth rind and a faintly nutty flavour.

Emmental The largest of the French cheeses with a firm texture and quite big holes. The flavour is quite mild.

Reblochon This dates back to the fourteenth century. It comes packed in small wooden boxes, each cheese weighing about 500g (1lb), with a pinkish-white skin and a delicate creamy flavour.

Tomme de Savoie Like all mountain areas, Savoie produces its own *tomme*, a low-fat cheese with a slightly grey rind and faintly salty taste. There are dozens of varieties, some marinated in the fiery liqueur *marc*.

Bleu de Gex-Haut-Jura From the immediate north, this is an excellent blue cheese with a slightly bitter taste. Other blue cheeses include Tignes, Sassanage, Sainte-Foy and Persillé du Mont-Cenis.

Other cheeses to look out for are those made from goat's milk like Bressan, Chevrotin d'Aravis, Chevrine de Lenta, tomme de Vercors and Picadon de l'Ardèche or de la Drôme. Persillé d'Aravis is blue goat's cheese.

Mild cheeses popular with children are the processed ones from Annecy, Beaumont which is like a Saint Paulin with a pale yellow rind and the various soft Vacherin cheeses.

Meat (*viande*)

These mountain districts rely heavily on pork (*porc*) for their daily fare. All sorts of cuts can be found including chops, cutlets and other easy-cook ways. Veal (*veau*) is quite common in Dauphiné, as well as turkey (*dinde*), while Savoie is famous for its mountain lamb (*agneau*), which is delicious. Chicken (*poulet*) is available everywhere and offal, especially lamb sweetbreads (*ris d'agneau*), liver (*foie*) and brains (*cervelles*) are popular in Savoie.

You may find some game on sale, mostly partridge (*perdreau*), pheasant (*faisan*), quail (*caille*) and woodcock (*bécasse*). Much of it is made into *pâtés de campagne*. Hare (*lièvre*) and wild rabbit (*lapin*) are also shot locally. It is obviously more practical to eat these in restaurants than deal with them in your self-catering apartment!

Fish (*poissons*)

The French Alps are a good area for fish, especially trout (*truite*), pike (*brochet*) and perch (*perche*). You may also come across the rarer freshwater burbot (*lotte des lacs*) which is a firm-fleshed fish rather like monkfish, as well as *lavaret*, a white-fleshed relation to the salmon, and *gravenche*, on sale in December. The freshwater shellfish called crayfish (*écrevisses*) should definitely be tried, as they are rarely found on sale in Britain. Like prawns, the tail is the part which is eaten.

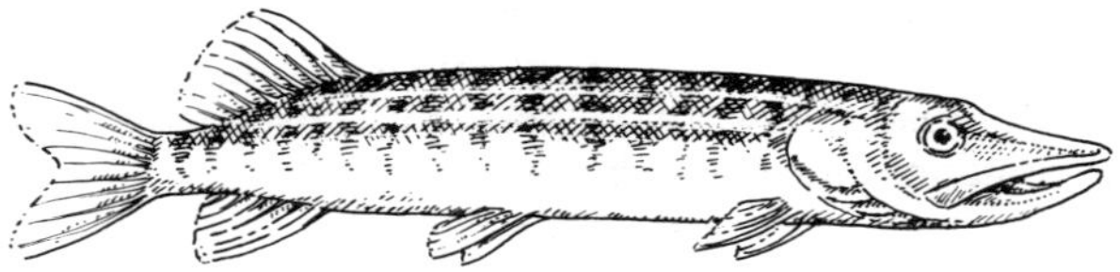

Pike

Fruit and Vegetables (*fruits et légumes*)

If you go summer glacier skiing, you get the best of both worlds: superb skiing and the best of the local fruit and vegetables this area is famous for. Savoie is renowned for its excellent strawberries (*fraises*), raspberries (*framboises*) and pears (*poires*). Cherries (*cerises*) and plums (*prunes*) are also grown locally. In winter, of course, soft fruit won't be available but you will still find pears and good apples (*pommes*), as well as chestnuts (*marrons or chataîgnes*). Walnuts (*noix*) are used not only for oil but in the pâtisserie as well (see below).

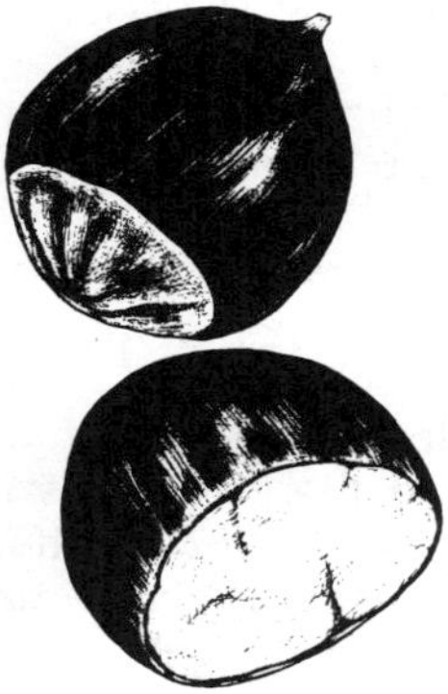

Chestnuts

The range of vegetables is pretty good, even in winter. Salad ingredients are obviously quite expensive being out of season, but root vegetables are plentiful, with potatoes (*pommes de terres*) and onions (*oignons*) in particular forming the base for many local hearty dishes. Other good winter vegetables are chard (*carde*), a kind of overgrown spinach with white stalks, and leeks (*poireaux*). You may find pumpkin (*potiron*) early in the season and garlic (*ail*) is good at this time of the year, choose a head which is firm with big cloves. Wild mushrooms are harvested locally — *cèpes* in late autumn, *morilles* and *mousserons* in spring.

Onions

Bread (*pain*)

If there is a separate bakery (*boulangerie*) in your resort, you can be pretty sure the bread is baked on the premises. The internationally known French stick (*baguette*) is, of course, on sale and good for picnic lunches. Don't forget *croissants* for breakfast and little *brioche* rolls. If you prefer brown bread go for the wholemeal *pain intégral* or *pain complet*, or try rye bread (*pain de siegle*). *Pain de campagne* doesn't go stale as quickly as the other types, but is quite hard and chewy.

Supermarkets rarely have as wide a choice as an individual baker, but do offer sliced factory bread if that's your passion.

PÂTISSERIE

Even the purpose-built resorts realise that supermarkets can't answer every need and there is almost always a pâtisserie within reach, sometimes with a café attached. If your fridge has a freezer tray, buy some locally made fruit sorbet for dessert (alternatively you can suspend it out of your window to keep frozen!). Winter skiers will have missed out on much of the summer fruits, but can buy some local jam (*confiture*), often made by the individual pâtisseries.

Nuts (*noisettes*), being a speciality of Savoie and Dauphiné, find their way into many of the local cakes. The light sponge cake *biscuit de Savoie* contains almonds, while *gâteau Grenoblais* is a rich walnut cake. There are quite a few macaroon and marzipan cakes because of all the almonds. Other goodies for snacks or tea are Pognes, large sweetened *brioches* filled or topped with fruit, courgette or even pumpkin.

Pâtisseries are also the places to find mouth-watering truffles and liqueur-filled chocolates from Chambéry. Chartreuse, raspberry liqueur or even honey are just some of the fillings. Finally, don't miss the wickedly rich Mont Blanc, a dessert made from puréed chestnuts, meringue and whipped cream.

3

FRENCH WINE

Unfortunately there is not room here to go into much detail about French wines, a subject which already fills many volumes, but I have tried to help you identify which ones you are most likely to drink when skiing. The French Alps stretch across Savoie and the mountainous north of Provence as well as being bordered by the Rhône valley and wines from all these regions can be found on the supermarket shelves in ski resorts, as well as labels from other parts of France like Bordeaux and Alsace.

One of the reasons French wine is so respected throughout the world is its strict quality control, something which is long-established but can be confusing for the newcomer. If you master the following terms, you should have a pretty good idea of the standard of wine you are paying for.

Vins de Pays are one up from *vins de table* and must be produced within the legally limited areas named on their labels. The type of vine and alcoholic strength must also be adhered to.

Vins Délimités de Qualité Supérieure (VDQS) are likewise from a defined area, and fall between *vins de pays* and AOC wines. The conditions of production are set down and can be legally enforced by the controlling board.

Appellation d'Origine Contrôlée (AOC or AC) — the production of wines which are granted an AOC classification is subject to even stricter scrutiny than the VDQS wines. Regulations cover not only area and production methods, but details like maximum yield per hectare, the pruning of the vines and the methods used in maturing vintages.

Savoie

Here the vineyards cling to the steep hillsides, and some years ripening conditions are far from perfect. The wines are mostly white, light and made to be drunk young, with the less good vintages tending to be rather thin and acidic. However, after a hard day's skiing, a carafe of crisp white Savoie wine is most refreshing, though it's not really good enough to make it worth taking home. Look out for the AOC Roussette wines like Roussette de Frangy, which are quite fruity yet still dry, and also Seyssel dry whites. Seyssel Mousseux is a light and pleasant sparkling white made by the champagne method. There are a few reds, most of which are light and fruity and served quite cold.

Something worth trying if you're in Savoie, for the experience if nothing else, is *vin jaune* from the neighbouring region of Jura. It is an intense, dry, sherry-like wine, drunk at a greater age than sherry and is quite expensive.

Rhône Valley (north)

Although these wines are not strictly local to the higher slopes of the Alpine area, they are of such good quality that it is worth seeking them out.

If you're feeling flush splash out on a bottle of Hermitage, but make sure it's around ten years old, when Hermitage wines reach their peak. The whites, which are not made in such quantity, are even more expensive. Red Crozes-Hermitage wine is the next best thing, and matures in about three to five years. Cornas red wine is really dark coloured and very fruity. Needing several years to reach perfection it is expensive and not that common.

A fairly good cheap country wine which you might try if you're skiing south-east of Grenoble is the AOC Côtes de Ventoux. This is a light red, rather like Beaujolais Nouveau with a fruity flavour.

The southern Rhône valley produces such classics as Châteauneuf-du-Pape, Gigondas and good quality AOC Côtes du Rhône. Côtes du Rhône Villages comes from the 17 communes allowed to include their name on the label. The dessert wine Beaumes de Venise also comes from around here.

Provence

Wine from the hot south of Provence was once made almost entirely for local consumption, but these days there are some good AOC wines being produced to be drunk after maturing for five or six years and those which filter north to the Alpine shops are worth trying. Look out for AOC Côtes de Provence rosé, Coteaux d'Aix en Provence, Coteaux des Baux-en-Provence (especially the reds) and Bandol, which are excellent reds from the very south.

OTHER DRINKS

Savoie makes good cider (*cidre*) from local apples. Beer is almost always of the lager (*bière blonde*) type; if you want a darker variety ask for *bière brune*.

An excellent dry vermouth from the area which has recently caught on in Britain is Chambéry, tasting faintly of herbs. Less well known are Chambéryzette, which is a similar drink flavoured with wild strawberries, and Génépy, another herby vermouth relation. Local liqueurs include one made from cherries and, from the Rhône valley, green and yellow Chartreuse, still made by the Carthusian monks from a seventeenth-century recipe naming 130 different herbs.

There are many manufacturers of fruit sirops around Grenoble. These, when diluted, make a pleasant soft drink and can also be added to cocktails. The famous Evian mineral water, made from glacier melt, is bottled on the shores of Lake Geneva.

4

REGIONAL DISHES IN THE FRENCH ALPS

As in the rest of France, in Savoie, Dauphiné and the Hautes Alpes you can find 'international' French cooking in every restaurant, and very good it is. But this is an area rich in its own specialities, so watch out for some of the regional dishes below. It is a major dairy-producing region, with plenty of cream and cheese used in cooking, but it also has excellent freshwater fish from the lakes and rivers. In summer it is a major fruit-growing centre.

The French Alps are bordered by the area around Lyons, famous for centuries for its gastronomy, the Rhône Valley, and, to the south, Provence. The influence of its neighbours can often be found in some of the dishes served locally.

RECIPES

Those dishes marked with an asterisk could be made while you are in the area. The others, being more complicated or requiring special equipment, are best left till you get home to try out. In the meantime, enjoy them in the local restaurants.

Soupe aux écrevisses (crayfish soup)
Gratin des écrevisses (crayfish in cheese sauce)
Quenelles de brochet (poached pike dumplings)
Pormonniers (Annecy sausages)*
Saucisses au vin blanc (pork sausages in white wine)*
Casserole Savoyarde (Savoy pork and sausage casserole)*

Escalopes de veau Savoyarde (Savoy veal escalopes)*
Gratin Dauphinoise (Dauphiné oven potatoes)*
Gratin Savoyarde (Savoy oven potatoes)*
Poires Savoyardes (Caramelised baked pears)*
Gâteau au noix (walnut cake)
Truffes au chocolat (chocolate truffles)

Crayfish soup
(soupe aux écrevisses)

Ideally the shellfish should be live for this, but you can make it with ready-cooked ones, although the flavour won't be quite as strong. Freshwater crayfish are quite difficult to buy in Britain, unless you live near a wholesale market, but scampi (Dublin Bay prawns) can be used instead. Serves 4.

8 crayfish
200 ml (7 fl oz) dry white wine
1 large carrot
1 medium leek
2 medium onions
2 tablespoons olive oil
1 tablespoon plain flour
1¾ litres (3 pints) water
bay leaf, parsley stalks, sprig thyme
piece lemon peel
seasoning
2 tablespoons double cream
1 egg yolk
1 tablespoon freshly chopped parsley

Bring the wine to the boil in a saucepan and drop in the crayfish, put on the lid and leave to simmer for 10 minutes. Strain and keep the wine in a bowl to one side. Clean and slice the leek, carrot and onions and sauté them in the hot oil in a saucepan for 5 minutes. Stir in the flour and cook for a minute then pour on the reserved wine, stirring until smooth, and the water. Add the herbs, lemon peel and seasoning and bring to the boil. Leave to simmer, uncovered, for 30 minutes.

Shell and chop the crayfish really finely. Strain the soup into another saucepan to remove the vegetables and add the crayfish to the liquid. Simmer, covered, over a low heat for 10 minutes. Beat the egg yolk with the cream, mix in a few tablespoons of the soup, then return this to the saucepan and heat through so it thickens slightly. Do not allow to boil.

Serve sprinkled with the chopped parsley.

Crayfish in cheese sauce
(gratin des écrevisses)

Another dish made from freshwater crayfish, this one makes a good main course. Again, scampi can be used. Serves 4.

24 cooked crayfish
750ml ($1\frac{1}{4}$ pints) water
300ml ($\frac{1}{2}$ pint) dry white wine
bay leaf, parsley stalks, black peppercorns, sprig thyme
1 medium onion
2 level tablespoons plain flour
2 tablespoons butter
200ml (7fl oz) milk
3 egg yolks
300ml ($\frac{1}{2}$ pint) double cream
seasoning
100g ($3\frac{1}{2}$oz) Gruyère cheese

Peel the crayfish and put the shells, heads, etc. into a saucepan with the water, white wine, herbs and peeled quartered onion. Bring to the boil and simmer for half an hour. Strain and set aside.

Make a roux with the butter and flour and gradually add the milk, plus an equal amount of the crayfish stock. Simmer, stirring occasionally, over a low heat for 5–10 minutes until thick. Beat the yolks well with the cream and stir into the sauce, seasoning well. Grate the cheese and stir this in too, keeping 2 tablespoons back.

Put the crayfish tails in a buttered, shallow, ovenproof dish, pour over the sauce and sprinkle with the rest of the cheese. Bake in an oven preheated to Gas 6/400°F/200°C for 30 minutes, until bubbling hot and golden brown.

Poached pike dumplings
(quenelles de brochet)

Traditionally, quenelles, which are light dumplings made of minced fish, had to be made by hand, which involved much time-consuming preparation. If you have a food processor, much of the work is taken out, and you can now make them at home as well as eating them in top French restaurants. You may use pike, trout or perch (all available in the French Alps), but not sea fish. Serves 6.

450g (1lb) filleted pike, trout, perch
3 tablespoons milk
200g (7oz) butter, preferably unsalted
8 slices white bread

3 tablespoons single cream
seasoning
2 whole eggs
2 egg yolks
little flour

First, put the skinned fish in the food processor and switch on until reduced to a minced purée. Melt the butter, add it to the fish, process, then remove the mixture and set aside. Cut the crusts from the bread and reduce it to really fine crumbs in the machine (no need to wash the bowl). Heat the milk and cream and pour on to the breadcrumbs. Mix well to a paste and season well. Add the eggs one at a time, with the machine running, and then the yolks. Finally, return the fish and bind the mixture together. Remove from the food processor and chill well for an hour at least.

Make the quenelles by rolling out the fish mixture with floured hands on a floured board, into a sausage shape. Divide the mixture into two or three to make it more manageable if you like. Cut off little sausages about the size and length of your thumb. Poach them in a large pan of boiling water or fish stock, being careful not to cook too many together or they stick to each other.

Serve with a prawn or lobster sauce or more simply, a cheese sauce with shelled prawns stirred in.

Pork sausages in white wine
(saucisses au vin blanc)

Here the sausages are browned first, and then served in a white wine sauce. The potatoes are cooked separately. Use the large sausages, rather than the chipolata size. Serves 4.

900g (2lb) good quality pork sausages
55g (2oz) butter
1 medium onion
2 cloves garlic
1 tablespoon flour
500ml (just under 1 pint) white wine
pinch thyme
seasoning

Put half the butter in a flameproof casserole dish or sauté pan and cook the sausages until brown all over, being careful not to burn the butter. Lift them out and set aside. Pour away the fat and then melt the rest of the butter. Finely chop the onion and cook gently in the butter with the crushed garlic until soft. Stir in the flour and then gradually add the wine, stirring all the time to prevent lumps forming. Add the thyme and some seasoning, cover the pan and simmer for 15 minutes.

Return the sausages to the pan and heat them through, then serve with sauté potatoes.

Annecy Sausages
(pormonniers)

Local herby sausages are used here with a large boiling sausage and potatoes, to make a simple supper dish you could easily knock together while on holiday in the area. Serves 6

1 large French pork boiling sausage
6 pormonniers
½ litre (1 pint) water
½ bottle white wine from Savoie
1kg (2¼lb) potatoes
seasoning

Bring the wine and water to the boil in a large saucepan, then throw in a little salt. Prick the pork sausage with a fork and add it to the liquid, and leave to simmer for 45 minutes. Peel the potatoes and cut them into large chunks. Prick the *pormonniers* in a similar fashion to prevent the skin splitting and add to the pan. Return to the boil, add the potatoes and simmer until these are cooked. Season well and serve very hot, accompanied by red wine.

Savoy pork and sausage casserole
(casserole Savoyarde)

Pork is the staple meat in the mountains of Savoie, and this warming hot pot uses chops, sausages (both smoked and fresh) and belly pork, padded out even further with cabbage. A really hearty dish for very hungry skiers. Serves 6–8

6-8 small pork chops
1 small smoked sausage
500g (1¼lb) smoked belly pork
1 French boiling sausage
2-3 sprigs thyme
sprig rosemary
bay leaf
seasoning
500ml (just under 1 pint) water
1¼kg (2¾lb) Savoy cabbage
2 large carrots
1 medium onion
2 tablespoons olive oil
sufficient water to blanch the cabbage

Slice the cabbage, bring it to the boil in a large pan of water and immediately drain. Slice the onion and the carrots and sauté them in a little oil in a large flameproof casserole or saucepan for 5 minutes. Add the blanched cabbage, lay the herbs over and then place the chops and pieces of belly pork on top. Season, pour in the water and bring to the boil. Leave to simmer for 45 minutes, then add the two different types of sausage and simmer a further 20 minutes.

Remove the meat. Pile the cabbage down on a hot serving platter, slice the sausages and belly pork and arrange on top with the chops.

Savoy veal escalopes
(escalopes de veau Savoyardes)

From the hearty peasant dish above to one made from prized veal, which passes the test in any haute cuisine restaurant, this takes just minutes to prepare. Serves 4

4 good-sized veal escalopes
2 tablespoons butter
seasoning
squeeze lemon juice
300ml (1/2 pint) double cream
150ml (1/4 pint) Chambéry or other dry vermouth

Beat the escalopes out really thin, or get the butcher to do this for you. Heat the butter in a large frying pan. Season the escalopes with salt, pepper and a squeeze of lemon juice, then add them to the pan as the butter starts to foam. Cook very briefly on both sides over a high heat before adding the Chambéry. Allow to cook until the liquid has reduced in volume, then add the cream, shaking the pan so the wine and cream blend together. Lower the heat and simmer for 3 or 4 minutes until the sauce starts to thicken and serve immediately.

It is better to serve vegetables on a separate plate so they don't end up drowned in the sauce.

Dauphiné oven potatoes
(gratin Dauphinoise)

This is the most famous of all French potato dishes – a filling, rich way of cooking them with cream. Controversy rages over the true ingredients; some recipes use milk and eggs instead of cream, others include grated cheese. Traditionally, cheese appears only in the Savoy version (see below).

The cooking time will vary according to how deep your dish is — the wider and shallower, the quicker it cooks. Serves 4–6

1 kg (2¼lb) waxy potatoes
1 clove garlic
2 tablespoons butter
seasoning
grated nutmeg (optional)
150 ml (¼ pint) milk
up to 450 ml (¾ pint) double cream

Peel the potatoes, and slice them very thinly lengthways. Peel the garlic and half crush it, then rub this around the inside of an earthenware gratin dish and discard. When the garlic juice has dried, rub the dish well with the soft butter. Layer the potatoes up in the dish, season well, adding a little grated nutmeg if you wish and pour on the milk. Add the cream until it reaches the top of the layers (allowing time for it to seep down) and place the dish in an oven preheated to Gas 5/375°F/190°C for about an hour. If the dish seems ready (it should be pretty solid) but still looks pale, turn the heat right up for a few minutes to brown the top.

Serve with a simply cooked piece of meat or fish.

Savoy oven potatoes
(gratin Savoyarde)

Similar to the Dauphinoise, only the cream and milk are replaced with beef stock, and cheese is included. Serves 4–6

1 kg (2¼lb) waxy potatoes
2 tablespoons butter
450 ml (¾ pint) beef stock
150 g (5 oz) Beaufort cheese

Peel and slice the potatoes as above. Butter the gratin dish, layer up the potatoes, interspersing the layers with grated cheese, finishing with cheese on top. Season well, pour over the hot stock and bake in an oven preheated to Gas 5/375°F/190°C for 45 minutes to an hour.

Caramelised baked pears
(poires Savoyardes)

Another dish using cream from Savoie, this time with pears as a dessert. You obviously wouldn't serve this if you were also having one of the potato dishes above! Serves 4

6 pears
3 tablespoons granulated sugar
2 tablespoons butter
3 tablespoons water
4 tablespoons double cream

Peel, quarter and core the pears. Put them in a shallow ovenproof dish, sprinkle with the sugar and dot with the butter. Shake the water over and bake in an oven preheated to Gas 7/425°F/220°C until the pears are tender and the juice is caramelised. Pour in the cream and serve.

Walnut cake
(gâteau au noix)

A delicious reminder of tea time at the *pâtisserie*, this is one of the easier and cheaper *gâteaux* to make. It uses no flour. Serves 8 or more

5 eggs
170g (6oz) castor sugar
170g (6oz) walnuts
4 tablespoons fine dried breadcrumbs
1 lemon
small pinch ground mace
little flour
250ml (½ pint) cream (for whipping)
apricot jam (optional)

Separate the eggs and beat the yolks with the sugar until thick and pale. Grate the rind from the lemon and add it together with the walnuts, finely chopped, the breadcrumbs and the mace. Whisk the egg whites till stiff but not dry and fold into the mixture.

Grease a 20cm (8in) cake tin and dust with flour. Shake out any excess, pour in the cake mixture and bake at Gas 2/300°F/150°C for 1–1¼ hours. When a skewer or knife inserted in the centre of the cake comes out clean, it is ready.

Turn out to cool on a wire rack then split in two, sandwich the halves together with whipped cream or jam (e.g. apricot) and cover the top and sides with whipped cream.

Chocolate truffles
(truffes au chocolat)

When you have finished up all the ones you've brought back with you, here is how to make your own delicious chocolate truffles. They are good served with coffee at the end of a meal. Good quality plain chocolate should be used – the best is the *pâtissier* sort. Makes about 30 truffles

225g (8oz) dark chocolate
6 tablespoons milk
1½ tablespoons unsalted butter
1½ tablespoons cognac
2 egg yolks
cocoa powder

Let the butter get to room temperature to soften it. Break the chocolate up into a bowl which will fit over a small pan of just simmering water. Add the milk and stir gently over the heat until the chocolate melts, then beat in the butter, a small knob at a time, keeping the bowl over the pan of water. When the mixture is completely smooth, remove from the heat and stir in the cognac.

Beat the egg yolks well and blend them into the chocolate mixture, then put the bowl in the fridge, with the surface of the mixture covered with greaseproof paper to prevent a crust forming, for about 3 hours.

It should now be firm enough for shaping. Take a teaspoon of it in your hands, roll into a ball and then shake in a paper bag with some cocoa powder until well coated. Best kept refrigerated.

SWITZERLAND

5

SHOPPING IN THE SWISS ALPS

Food in Switzerland is almost invariably of a very high standard and in many areas you are spoilt for choice. Self-caterers are particularly well looked after – don't forget that Switzerland is the home of such well-known names as Nestlé, Maggi and Knorr, all of whom led the world in introducing us to convenience foods like packet soups and sauces, stock cubes and so on. These are generally of a higher standard than those found in Britain, and have a more imaginative range of products with a slightly more gourmet slant.

Unfortunately for us, the strong Swiss economy and high standard of living also means that the country has become extremely expensive for British tourists. If you are considering choosing Switzerland for your skiing holiday, don't think it will be *cheap* just because you are doing your own cooking. On the other hand many resorts have superb skiing and unbeatable après-ski life and 'atmosphere'. So long as you have worked out your finances and planned carefully where you can save money on the food side, you'll have a great time.

Even if you are flying, it is worth trying to squeeze in as much as possible in the way of small bags of herbs, seasonings, tea bags, coffee (in plastic bags) and so on. You will be spending enough on other things without splashing out on items you won't use up but are useful to have by the stove. If you are taking the car, this is the one time I would recommend loading it with food – although you will then miss out on the delicious Swiss-made goodies like their excellent jams, so leave a bit of room for flexibility.

Many resorts have supermarkets, where everything is displayed beautifully, particularly on the mouth-watering delicatessen counter. The older traditional villages will still have a butcher, baker, pâtisserie or cake shop and so on.

SUPERMARKET AND GROCER
(Supermarché et épicerie/Supermarkt und Lebensmittelgeschäft)

Tinned food is of good quality and generally comes in medium cans of around 425g (about 15oz). Local specialities to look for are tinned *rösti* (a potato dish), various mushrooms like *cèpes (steinpilze)* and *chanterelles (eierschämme)* which make tastier omelettes than the familiar button mushrooms. You can also find tinned goulash soup and red cabbage.

Tinned *canneloni* and *ravioli* make good quick supper dishes, and baked bean fans will be pleased to hear there is a variety available in Switzerland too. French beans, tiny peas and carrots are all available in tins, as are pulses like lentils, red kidney beans and butter beans. These are excellent for stews and casseroles and mean you can avoid the soaking and long cooking of the dried variety. Hilco, a Liechtenstein firm, has a very good selection of all of these.

Red peppers, beetroot, oriental salad and mexican salad containing sweetcorn are all available in jars as well as tiny pickled onions (the silverskin variety) and gherkins.

Swiss jam is absolutely delicious and worth bringing home. Varieties include redcurrant, blackberry, plum, strawberry, apricot, raspberry, red cherry and, my favourite, black cherry. Héro is a good name to look out for. The Swiss have been

Jams

streets ahead of the rest of us in the field of packet food, sauces and so on for years. Apart from the famous stock cubes and all-purpose seasoning like Aromat (good for sprinkling on steaks and escalopes as well as adding to salads and stews), you can find pretty good sauces. These either come in handy small jars or packets. This is the one time I don't frown too heavily on using a packet sauce, even the white or cheese ones can be improved by adding some mustard or chopped cooked onion or fresh herbs. Don't forget the role of packet soups in creating easy casserole sauces, especially if you use the 'cream of' variety. Gautsch produce a pack of 5 sauces in jars, ideal for serving with a beef fondue: barbecue, curry, mousseline, bourguignonne and tartare.

Mayonnaise, tomato purée, garlic purée and simple liver pâtés are all available in tubes – a non-messy and non-wasteful addition to sandwiches for packed lunches.

Pasta and rice (*pâtes et riz/Nudeln und Reis*)

Most of the different sizes and shapes of pasta are available dried in packets (see Shopping in Italy for descriptions). Allow about 90g (3oz) per person for a pasta with sauce dish, slightly less if you're serving it as an accompaniment to a main course. While the strand varieties like *spaghetti* and *tagliatelle* are good for main courses, the little stars and shells are ideal for adding to a hearty soup. Twists and other shapes of a more manageable length are best for serving as a side dish.

Long grain rice, both white and less commonly brown, and risotto rice are both available. Study the packet well; the easy-cook variety requires slightly less cooking time.

Vegetables and fruit (*légumes et fruits/Gemüse und Obst*)

These are on sale in the small supermarkets and grocers. Even in small resorts there is a surprisingly good selection of vegetables, including aubergines (*aubergines/Eierfrucht*), radicchio (excellent in salads), and fennel (*fenouil/Fenchel*). There is always a good choice of root vegetables like carrots (*carottes/Möhren*), swedes (*chou navet/Streckrüben*), and potatoes (*pommes de terre/Kartoffeln*), as well as celery (*céleri/Sellerie*), and red and white cabbage (*chou/Kohl*). Items like garlic (*ail/Knoblauch*) and ginger (*gingembre/Ingwer*) can be found to spice up meat dishes and there is always quite a variety of salad ingredients.

Fresh fruit is in more limited supply, although you will

always find oranges (blood oranges in winter), grapes (*raisins/Trauben*) and bananas (*bananes/Bananen*), and a couple of sorts of apples (*pommes/Äpfeln*).

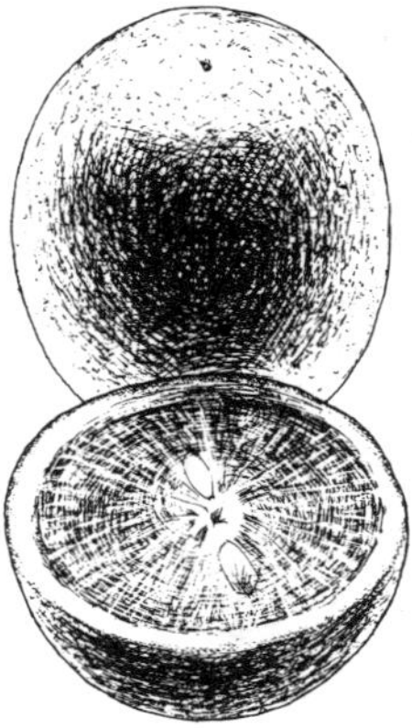

Oranges

CHEESE (*fromage/Käse*)

Switzerland's image abroad rests on cheese and watches, although the monopoly has been broken on both and you can now buy so-called Emmentaler cheese as far away as Argentina and Australia. Because of foreign competition, Switzerland is working harder than ever to keep its standards high. A recent government decree has gone out specifying the exact size the holes in a Gruyère should reach (only the Swiss could be so precise). Times for maturing and the weight of the loaf are also regulated by law.

Emmental This massive cheese with the familiar cherry-sized holes is ivory coloured and slightly grainy. Emmental is made in all the Swiss–German cantons and has a full, slightly nutty flavour.

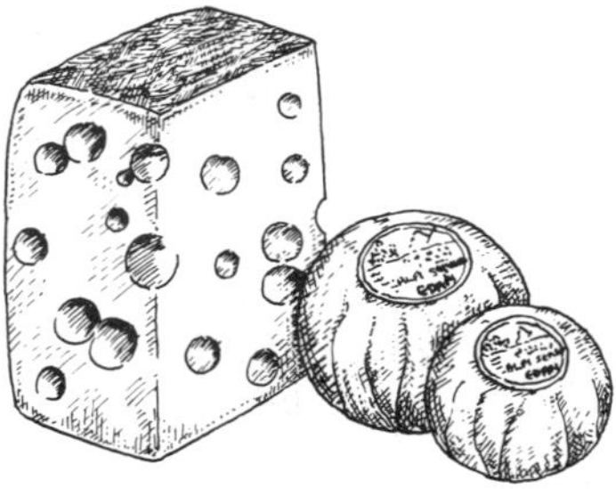

Cheeses

Gruyère (Greyerzer) Similar to an Emmental but softer textured and sharper tasting, with a stronger aroma.

Sbrinz This is produced in central Switzerland. It is a hard variety, ideal for grating with a strong taste and does not melt into strings like Gruyère, which makes it a good cheese for seasoning sauces and so on.

Royalp This smooth, fresh-tasting creamy soft cheese is quite a new one on the Swiss scene, first being made at the turn of the century. It is easy to cut and quite mild, yet with a good flavour.

Appenzell Another soft cheese, this one is rubbed with white wine and spices during maturation, which gives it its special sharp, slighty tangy flavour.

Schabziger/Sapsago This is a soft cheese made from curdled milk, finely ground and mixed with powdered herbs before being shaped into little cone shapes known as 'Stöckli'. It is better suited to filling rolls or eating with a glass of wine after dinner, than cooking.

Vacherin Mont d'Or and Vacherin Fribourgeois These are lovely soft milky cheeses from the French-speaking part of the country.

Tommes Vaudoises These little 'cakes' of cheese, weighing only about 125g (4½oz) and quite reasonably priced, are a good addition to a packed lunch.

Raclette Originally from the valleys of Valais, this easy-melting cheese is now in great demand everywhere, being ideally suited to the making of the traditional Raclette dish.

MEAT (*viande/Fleisch*)

Even small places often have a separate butcher (*boucherie/Fleischerei* or *Metzgerei*), where you will find the meat of high quality but pretty pricey. The cheapest is chicken (*poulet/Huhn*), available jointed or whole, followed by pork (*porc/Schweinefleisch*). Look out for spare ribs cut in the Chinese way, which make a good cheap dish. Beef (*boeuf/Rind-fleisch* is very good but extremely expensive (including mince), and veal (*veau/Kalbfleisch*) can soon empty your wallet too, though the escalopes are widely available, and a good buy for casseroles is the diced braising veal. A local speciality is the dried beef (*viande séchée/Bundnerfleisch*) and air-cured meats like Délices de Grison, which you should ask for sliced paper thin for extra value. Even so, it is actually cheaper to take salami and so on from Britain than buy it out there!

Chinese-style spare ribs

BAKERY (*boulangerie/Bäckerei*)

You will find a bakery a natural part of any Swiss village, where dozens of different sorts of bread (*pain/Brot*) are baked on the premises every day. There are loaves similar to our crusty cottage or farmhouse ones, the familiar French sticks, rye bread, as well as plaits, rolls, croissants, sweet bread, wholemeal and half-white half-brown varieties. If you try a different sort every day you still won't have worked your way around the shop. Swiss bread tends to go stale quicker than the sort we are used to in England, so seal yours in a carrier or plastic bag with a rubber band.

Don't miss trying croissants filled with a little soft chocolate, which are terrific for mid-morning snacks or tea. Watch out, though, they could become addictive!

Many bakeries have a *pâtisserie* section as well, called the *Konditerei*, where you can pick up a mouth-watering selection of wonderfully fattening cakes and pastries, often covered in masses of whipped cream. If you prefer less rich food, you can buy very good flans (*tartes/Torten*) topped with apple, plum or other fruits.

Croissants and plait

6
SWISS WINE

If you are going on holiday to Switzerland, now is the chance to taste its wines, for they are not exported in any great quantity and are very rarely found in Britain. This is not because they are poor quality, or don't 'travel well', far from it. Due to Switzerland's mountainous terrain, not much land is available for wine-growing (although you do see vineyards clinging to slopes that most people would think twice about walking along). The majority of the harvest is therefore kept by the canny Swiss for their own consumption. There is a good variety, although you will find that most of the wine tends towards the delicate and light rather than the robust, with a fragrant bouquet and refreshing taste. Whites outstrip the reds, although the Italian-speaking region concentrates on the latter.

The four main wine-producing areas are in the French- and Italian-speaking areas. A few scattered small vineyards are found in the German-speaking part.

Le Valais

This deep sheltered valley at the headwaters of the river Rhône near the border with France is Switzerland's most famous wine-producing region. Look out for the dry yet fruity Fendant wine made from the Chasselas grape; this is one of the most popular national labels. This area also produces Johannisberg from the Sylvaner grape which has a delicate flavour and full body. Malvoisie is known for its subtle sweetness, and the best red from the area is Dôle, usually a blend of Pinot Noir and Chardonnay grapes, which is pleasantly full-bodied. A Dôle made purely from Pinot Noir grapes, which give a rich velvety flavour, is considered to be of the highest quality.

Lake Geneva (Lac Léman)

This is split into two areas, Mandement and Vaud. The former lies just north of the city of Geneva. Here the Chasselas grape harvest is turned into a good range of fruity and often slightly sparkling white wines called Perlan. In a more expensive price bracket you will find rarer wines made from the Riesling and Sylvaner grapes as well as the Aligote and Chardonnay. For those who like rosé, try some from the Gamay grape. Swiss rosés are light and not at all sweet.

Vaud consists of three districts all of which concentrate on white wines, which are called Dorin. These are mild and fruity and good for everyday drinking. From Chablais, upstream from where the river Rhône flows into Lake Geneva, you find good wines from villages like Aigle, Yvorne, Ollon and Bex. Further along, between Geneva and Lausanne, the area known as La Côte has a number of excellent wines from the villages of Bougy, Mont-sur-Rolle, Vinzel and Féchy. Further east still, in the Lavaux district east of Lausanne, the vineyards cling to precipitous southfacing hillsides on endless narrow terraces. Villages like Cully, St Saphorin, Epesses and Dezaley are all names to look out for.

Vaud also produces some good quality fragrant reds called Salvagnin.

Neuchâtel

Unlike most Swiss wines, those from the lime-rich slopes surrounding lakes Neuchâtel, Bienne and Morat are sent for export as well as being drunk locally, which means these are the ones foreigners are more likely to have come across. Most of them are white, often with a slight sparkle, although there is a light red produced as well. The most famous Neuchâtel wine is the crisp dry rosé made from the Pinot Noir grape. Its name, Oeil de Perdrix, is an ancient wine term denoting the pink colour of a partridge's eye.

Ticino

This southern region of Switzerland, where Italian is the first language, produces full bodied, deep-coloured heady red wines, mostly from the Merlot grape. They are good for drinking with steak and *fondue bourguignonne*, but not widely found outside the immediate area.

Other much smaller wine-growing areas are scattered throughout the German-speaking cantons of Switzerland. They are very much local wines, consumed in the immediate vicinity and not on sale much elsewhere. Ones to look out for if you're in the area are those made from the Pinot Noir and Riesling–Sylvaner grapes in the cantons of St-Gall, the Grisons, Thurgovia, Schaffhausen and Zurich.

OTHER DRINKS

Swiss beer (*bière/Bier*) is the lager type, available on draught or bottled. Imported labels are also popular, though rather more expensive, and come mainly from Germany or Alsace. Like Austria, Switzerland has a good selection of fruit brandies, a clear strong liquid bearing names like *pomme* (apple), *pruneau* (plum) and *kirsch* (cherry). Watch out for Poire William, a pear brandy which often has a whole pear encased inside the bottle. *Marc* is made from the final pressings of grapes and constitutes a fairly lethal *eau-de-vie*.

Mineral water is often drunk throughout meals and is available still or sparkling. Natural juices are also popular; try grape juice (*jus de raisin/Traubensaft*).

7

REGIONAL DISHES IN THE SWISS ALPS

Eating out in Switzerland, whether it be an haute cuisine meal with corresponding staggering prices or a simple mountain-side snack, is rarely a disappointing experience. Service is friendly and efficient and, although you can get international-style dishes nearly everywhere, most resort restaurants use local ingredients to prepare delicious traditional meals as well.

If you want to keep costs down go for the *plat de jour* or *assiette de jour*, a single filling dish which changes daily. Many restaurants also do a fixed price meal of two or more courses, sometimes including a glass of wine. After ordering, slips from the cash till will be placed under your plate or on a small saucer on your table. At the end of the meal the waiter will add these up and tell you the total amount.

Portions are pretty large, but bear in mind that in some restaurants it is normal to serve a similar-sized second helping, on a clean plate. While you peruse the menu, look around other tables and see if this is the custom in the place you have chosen.

Economy meals include very good pizzas and big plates of pasta with a warming sauce. Service charge is included in prices unless otherwise indicated, but sometimes you may want to leave a few coins as well.

RECIPES

Those dishes marked with an asterisk could be made while you are in the area. The others, being more complicated or requiring special equipment, are best left till you get home to try out. In the meantime, enjoy them in the local restaurants. Many of the names are in the Swiss German dialect, which should help you identify them more easily when you are in Switzerland!

Schoppa da Jotta (barley soup)*
Cholermüs (mountain omelette)*
Rösti (fried grated potato)*
Fondue Neuchâtel (cheese fondue)
Fondue Bourguignonne (steak fondue)
Eglifilets in Weisswein (perch in white wine)*
Emincé Zurichoise (Zurich veal)*
Raclette (melted cheese slices)
Tarte aux pruneaux (open plum flan)
Délices de Grison (air cured beef)*
Consommé aux oeufs/Eiersuppe (broth with egg)
Toggeburger (Swiss hamburger)
Steak Tartar

Barley soup
(Schoppa da Jotta)

Barley can be cultivated under almost any conditions and has a short growing period, which explains its tremendous popularity in mountainous areas of Switzerland. This traditional soup is the best-known dish from the Graubünden canton and makes an excellent lunch with a basket of local bread. Try this recipe when you get home if you are near a supplier of smoked beef. Serves 6

500g (1¼lb) thick piece smoked beef
175g (6oz) pearl barley
1 small head cabbage
225g (8oz) potatoes
1 tablespoon flour (optional)
3 tablespoons cream
1½ litres (2¾ pints) water
seasoning
1 tablespoon freshly chopped parsley

Put the piece of beef into the water with the barley. Bring to the boil and simmer, covered, for 2 hours. Finely shred the cabbage, peel and dice the potatoes, add them, and simmer for another hour. By now the soup should be pretty thick. Should it require further thickening, beat the flour into the cream and stir it in, otherwise add the cream alone. Remove the beef, cut it into small cubes and return to the pan with a little seasoning if needed. A spoonful of chopped parsley livens up the appearance.

Mountain Omelette
(Cholermüs)

This is a very traditional dish from the Swiss Alps, once a staple dish of the self-sufficient herdsmen, using ingredients they produced themselves. It would make an excellent breakfast before a day's skiing. Do not use a non-stick frying pan or the cutting you do while cooking will damage the coating of the pan. Serves 2

6 tablespoons plain flour
3 eggs
butter
400ml (3/4 pint) cream or milk (or half-half)
large pinch salt

Put the flour in a bowl and gradually beat in the eggs and then the cream or milk to form a thick batter. Leave to stand for about 30 minutes then melt the butter in a frying pan. Pour in the batter and cook without stirring until the bottom is golden brown. Then turn the omelette-pancake over and immediately start cutting it up with a knife or spoon as it cooks. Cook until lightly browned all over.

You can serve it plain with a little sugar or cinnamon, dipped in milk, or with stewed apples or pears.

Fried grated potato
(Rösti)

This is a cheap, filling and very traditional Swiss dish, found throughout the country, although it originated in Bern. It is still sometimes eaten for breakfast among the herding communities of the northern and central Alps. Here is the basic recipe, followed by some variations. Serves 4–6

1kg (2 1/4lb) potatoes
salt
lard, dripping or oil for cooking

Parboil the potatoes in their skins until they are partly

cooked but still quite firm when you pierce them with a fork. Drain, cool, peel and grate them (or use the special *rösti* shredders on sale) or slice into shreds, sprinkle with salt. Heat the fat (you could use oil but lard or dripping gives a better flavour) in a heavy-bottomed frying pan, add the potatoes and brown for about half an hour over a low heat, turning occasionally. Near the end of frying time compress the mass with a spatula and continue to fry until a firm crust has formed. Shake loose and turn out onto a plate. Cut like a cake.

There are many regional variations on *rösti*, the more elaborate turning it into quite a substantial meal by itself if served with a good salad. If you like you can be inventive and lay a slice of ham on top, cover with cheese, melt this then slide a fried egg on top.

Here are some regional differences:

Appenzell. With elbow-shaped macaroni, diced bacon and Appenzeller cheese.

Basel. With onion rings.

Bern. With diced bacon and milk.

Glarus. With Schabziger cheese.

Ticino. With diced bacon and rosemary.

Uri. With mountain cheese and onions, dunked in *café au lait*.

Western Switzerland. With bacon, tomatoes, paprika and Gruyère.

Zurich. With chopped onion and caraway.

Cheese fondue
(Fondue Neuchâtel)

The word *fondue* comes from the French *fondre*, which means to melt, and this dish appears to be just that – melted cheese, into which you dip pieces of bread on long skewers. But the Swiss will tell you there is much more to it than meets the eye, and it is certainly the case that an inexpertly made *fondue* can cause indigestion.

If making it at home, you should always use the correct cheese (available by mail from the Swiss Centre in London if not locally), the driest of white wines and a dash of Kirsch. And do follow the advice of the Swiss and drink white wine with a cheese *fondue* – red wine, lots of beer, or, worst of all, water will not aid the digestion! Non-drinkers should stick to lemon or herb tea. A cheese *fondue* should be made in a fire-proof casserole dish with one strong handle (the Le Creuset ones are ideal) called a *caquelon* and then kept hot over a small spirit lamp. Serves 4

1 clove garlic
450 ml (3/4 pint) dry white wine
2 1/2–3 1/2 cups grated Emmentaler cheese
2 1/2–3 1/2 cups grated Gruyére cheese
1 liqueur glass Kirsch
1 heaped teaspoon cornflour
black pepper
pinch grated nutmeg
French bread stick (1/2–1 day old)

Peel and halve the garlic clove then rub it around the dish before discarding. Put the dish on the stove and heat the wine, then slowly add the cheese, stirring constantly. Bring to the boil over a medium heat. Dissolve the cornflour in the Kirsch and pour into the cheese. Simmer briefly to thicken, add the pepper and nutmeg, then remove to a small burner and start the meal.

Put a couple of baskets of cubed French bread on the table. Pierce each piece of bread with a proper *fondue* fork and dip it in the hot cheese before eating. Stir the dish occasionally.

Steak fondue
(Fondue Bourguignonne)

This is made by dipping pieces of prime steak into a cauldron of hot oil, again at the table. Personally I prefer it to cheese *fondue*, and although the meat may be expensive you will be surprised by how far it stretches.

Allow about 150–175 g (5–6 oz) per head of rump or fillet steak. Fill a metal *fondue* pan no more than half full with vegetable or sunflower oil. Heat over the stove until a cube of bread browns when dropped in, then light the spirit lamp and transfer the pan very carefully. It is advisable not to dip too many pieces of meat in at once. Have a selection of sauces available to dunk the meat in after cooking – tartar, barbecue, mustard mayonnaise, ketchup – whatever takes your fancy. It is important not to eat the meat straight from your skewer or you will burn your lips badly – transfer it to a fork first.

Tradition says that those who lose the 'cargo' from their skewer must pay some kind of forfeit!

You may well come across other kinds of *fondue* as well, like Chinese *fondue* where you cook pieces of pork and veal in a pot of simmering stock and then dip them in spicy oriental sauces. At the end of the meal you crack an egg into the stock, whisk it lightly and drink the stock as a soup.

Perch in white wine
(Eglifilets in Weisswein)

Since Switzerland is landbound, seafish are not a common part of the Swiss diet. Freshwater fish like perch and trout, however, are very popular. They are caught both in the lakes and in mountain streams. Perch is definitely woth seeking out while you are in Switzerland; it has been praised by gourmets throughout the ages for its delicate flavour. Serves 6

1kg (2¼lb) fresh perch fillets
seasoning
lemon juice
Worcestershire sauce
flour for coating
300ml (½ pint) double cream
4 tablespoons butter
250ml (8fl oz) good quality dry white wine
pinch dried thyme
170g (6oz) button mushrooms
1 tablespoon fresh chopped parsley

Skin the perch fillets and rub them with seasoning, lemon juice and a very little Worcestershire sauce. Lightly flour them and fry in the butter over a medium heat. Meanwhile, mix the cream with the wine in a saucepan, season and add the thyme, and simmer together for 5 minutes.

Wipe the mushrooms and slice very thinly. Transfer the cooked perch fillets to a warm serving dish, scatter the mushrooms down the centre and pour the very hot sauce over the top. Sprinkle with parsley and serve.

Zurich veal
(Emincé Zurichoise)

The Swiss version of Boeuf Stroganoff, this calls for good quality veal. Some recipes use plain instead of soured cream, but I prefer the latter, especially as veal can sometimes be a bit bland. If you want to try it at home or in your self-catering apartment, it's extremely quick to prepare. Use wild mushrooms if you can find them on sale; they are much tastier. If you can't find sour cream, add a squeeze of lemon juice to normal cream a few minutes before using. Serves 4

700g (1½lb) veal fillet or boned cutlets
flour for coating
3 tablespoons butter
½ medium onion, sliced
50g (2oz) mushrooms, sliced
150ml (¼ pint) white wine
seasoning
150ml (¼ pint) sour cream

Slice the veal into matchstick strips and dust with a little flour. Heat the butter in a frying pan and when it is sizzling throw in the onion and mushrooms and sauté till soft. Add the veal and stir-fry for about a minute over a high heat. Remove the meat and let it drain in a sieve while you make the sauce. Add the wine and seasoning to the pan, simmer for a couple of minutes then stir in the cream and meat. Heat through without boiling and serve with rice, noodles or *rösti*.

Raclette

Another easy and informal meal, which just requires the right ingredients and (preferably) an open fire for a successful evening. You need a large piece of Raclette cheese (restaurants do it with half a whole 'loaf', but 3½kg (7½lb) is a bit big for the average household!). Hold it in front of the fire on a sturdy toasting fork, or even propped on a fireproof table or stool. When it begins to melt, slice off the outer layer, which should be crispy on the outside, transfer this to a plate, serve and start again. In some places you can buy special cheese slicers which look a bit like a violin bow, where the wire cuts through the cheese like butter.

Raclette is served with plainly boiled potatoes, in their skins, and is accompanied by dishes of gherkins, pickled onions and sour plum — washed down of course with a good local dry white wine.

Open plum flan
(tarte aux pruneaux)

In Swiss *pâtisseries* you will find everything from *croissants au chocolat* to whipped cream *gâteaux* and beautiful open fruit flans. Here's the recipe for one of the flans, using dark plums. Serves 6

225g (8oz) plain flour
pinch salt
40g (1½oz) caster sugar
150g (5oz) butter
1 egg yolk
2 tablespoons iced water
25g (1oz) ground almonds
75g (3oz) sponge cake crumbs
1kg (2¼lb) dark purple plums
25g (1oz) caster sugar
squeeze lemon juice
2 tablespoons butter
up to 225g (8oz) apricot jam
icing sugar

Make a sweet shortcrust pastry by sifting the flour and salt into a bowl, stirring in the sugar and rubbing in the cold butter. Add the egg yolk and water and knead to a smooth dough. Chill for 30 minutes. Meanwhile quarter and stone the plums.

Roll out the pastry on a floured board and line a greased 23cm (9in) flan tin. Scatter the almonds and crumbs over the base then arrange the plums in circles until full. Sprinkle with the sugar and a squeeze of lemon juice, dot with butter and bake in a pre-heated oven at Gas 6/400°F/200°C for 30 minutes, until the pastry is golden brown and the plums soft.

Melt the jam in a saucepan with a spoonful of water to form a glaze and brush all over the flan. Cool. Sieve a little icing sugar over the plums just before serving.

Air-cured beef
(*délices de Grison*)

Literally translated as delights from Grison, these slices of air-cured beef and ham from the Swiss mountains make an appetite-teasing starter as well as good sandwich fillings. It's pretty expensive (as are all cured and smoked meats in the Alps), so ask the shop to slice it extra thin. Serve with a little frilly-leaved lettuce mixed with a sliced chicory head, dressed in a faintly mustardy vinaigrette.

Broth with egg
(consommé aux oeufs/Eiersuppe)

This makes frequent appearances on Swiss restaurant menus and you either like the idea of an egg floating around in your soup or you don't. The important things is to ask for it really hot, then when you break into the egg and whisk it in it will cook in strands, rather than staying a rather off-putting gelatinous texture. Very good for those who are feeling a bit off-colour, or who are trying to watch their weight.

Swiss hamburger
(Toggeburger)

The Swiss have shown their patriotism by coming up with this alternative name for the ubiquitous hamburger. Their version is more like those you find in America than in an English supermarket, however, made from 100 per cent good quality chopped beef, grilled and served with good chips (*frites*) and a variety of sauces or melting Swiss cheese.

Steak Tartar

This must be made from top quality beef or it will be very chewy and extremely unpleasant. Consequently it is an expensive dish to order when eating out, but fans of steak tartar will be pleased to hear it is quite popular and therefore not too hard to find in Swiss restaurants.

ITALY

8

SHOPPING IN THE ITALIAN ALPS

Italy once had a reputation for being a very cheap place to eat well. As the national standard of living has risen this is becoming less true, though prices are certainly lower than what we are used to paying. Unlike France, which has a number of purpose-built ski resorts, most Italian skiing destinations are built around an existing village or small town with a thriving community all year round. This means that if there is a supermarket, there will still be a good selection of small specialist shops which are much better for tracking down the best local produce.

SUPERMARKET (*supermercato*)

Italy is good for tinned food, the most famous being tomatoes (*pomodori*), but look out too for canned tuna (*tonno*)

Chickpeas

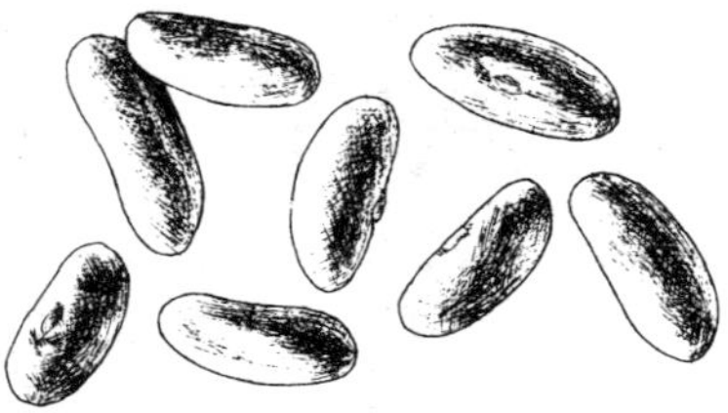

Cannellini beans

and anchovies (*alici* or *acciughe*) which are good for making into quick pasta sauces or salads. You can also get anchovies and tuna loose from barrels on the delicatessen counter. Choose tuna marked *ventresca* (stomach) which is the best part.

Dried herbs and spices are readily available — rosemary (*rosmarino*) is a good pungent one to liven up casseroles — along with packet soups, tubes of anchovy, garlic (*aglio*), onion (*cipolle*) and tomato purée, ready-made sauces for pasta dishes and ketchup. There will be a good selection of dried pulses like chickpeas (*ceci*), small white *cannellini* beans, red or speckled *borlotti* and so on, but these need to be soaked overnight and then require one to two hours simmering until tender, so you may prefer to pay a little more and buy tinned ones which are ready to eat. They are excellent for padding out casseroles, adding to soups (like minestrone) and making into easy salads with a pungent olive oil and garlic dressing.

Olive oil (*olio d'oliva*) is of course a staple of Italian cooking. The best is from Lucca in Tuscany (watch out for the name on the label) and the high grade bottles are expensive, but cheaper than in Britain so worth taking home. The greener the oil, the stronger tasting and heavier it will be. Italians use it for cooking as well as salads, but you may find this a bit rich and prefer to use sunflower oil (*olio de sasso*) for frying, which is widely available and much cheaper. If you have children, tinned fruit like peaches (*pesche*), pears (*pere*) and fruit 'cocktails' will be popular, especially in the more remote resorts which in mid-winter will have limited supplies of fresh fruit. Tinned *ravioli*, *cannelloni* and other pastas are also available in cans, but it seems a shame to resort to this in the country which is the home of pasta, particularly if you can get it fresh (see below).

Even small supermarkets usually have a reasonable supply of frozen foods, including seafood meals, pizza dough and clams (*vongole*) which are good included in a pasta sauce. Frozen vegetables available include broad and French beans (*fave* and *fagioini verde*), peas (*piselli*), spinach (*spinaci*) and broccoli (*broccoli*).

Fish (*pesce*), which apart from trout (*trota*) is rarely available fresh in the mountains, can be bought frozen from supermarkets. Apart from fishfingers, which children will be pleased to hear have reached even the Alps, you can get frozen hake (*merluza*), squid (*calamari*), prawns (*gamberi*) and shrimps (*gamberetti*). Hake is a good white fish that can be cooked in much the same way as a piece of haddock or cod. You will also find chicken, veal, pork chops and even delicacies like quail in the freezer cabinet.

Pasta and rice

There is such a choice of this it needs a section to itself. Below are listed the different names given to the most common of the dozens of shapes used in pasta-making. In a shop you can just pick it up off the shelf if buying dried, or point if going for the fresh variety, which is delicious and much quicker to cook (cuts down on the steam in your apartment!), but it's handy to know the different names when you are eating out. Fresh pasta is often sold vacuum packed, which doesn't mean you can keep it indefinitely, but lengthens its life somewhat.

Cannelloni Tubes of pasta used for stuffing with meat and vegetables.

Conchiglie (conch shells) Shell shapes; another variation are called *maruzze* (seashells).

Farfalle (butterflies) Bow-shaped pasta pieces.

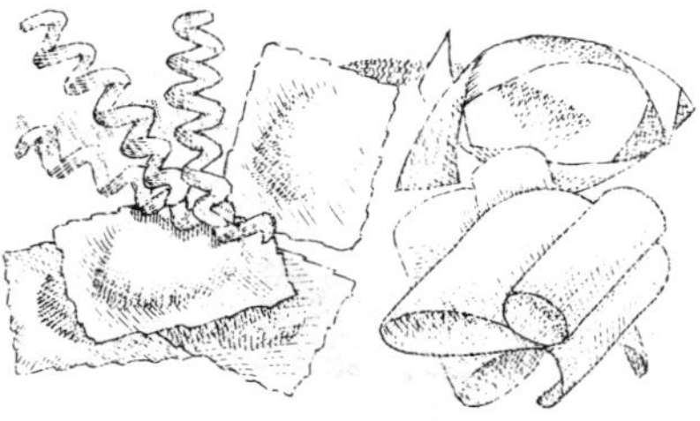

A selection of pasta

Fettuce Flat noodles, wider than *tagliatelle* (see below). *Fettucine* is the Roman version, narrower but thicker than *tagliatelle.*

Lasagne Broad sheets of pasta, coloured green with spinach used for layering up with bolognese sauce and cheese sauce.

Maccheroni Small tubes of pasta, of which the narrower version is called *maccheroncini.*

Ravioli Stuffed squares of pasta.

Rigatoni Large ridged tubes of pasta.

Tagliatelli Long flat egg noodles about 2cm (¾in) wide, often served alone with meat dishes.

Tortellini Stuffed knot-shaped pasta pieces.

In addition there are several kinds used in soups, usually very small and with names like *capelli d'angelo* (angel hair), *stellini* (little stars) and *ditalini* (little thimbles).

Although pasta is eaten all over Italy, it is essentially a southern dish. For northerners, rice is the staple food, grown in the fertile Po Valley. It is served as a starter, in soups, salads, meat dishes, even in desserts. For risotto-making you need to buy the shorter-grained variety called Arborio.

DELICATESSEN (*alimentari,salumeria*)

Every town will have one of these and it is a treasure trove for discovering the best of Italian food as well as the local specialities. If you're making up packed lunches to take out for the day, a stop off here is essential. In larger towns you

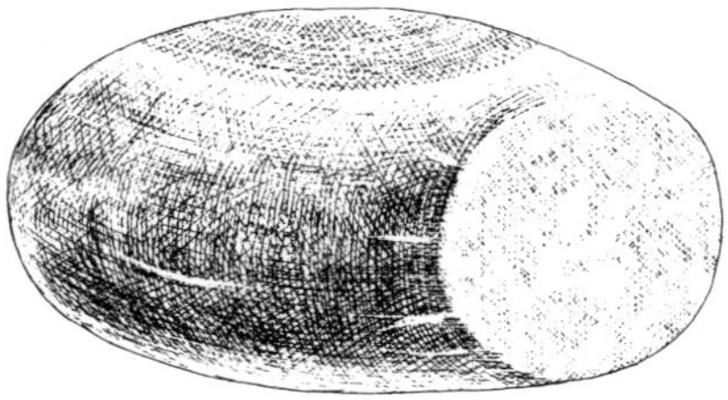

Mortadella sausage

may also be able to buy cheese in a specialist cheese shop and things like milk, yoghurt and butter from a dairy (*latteria*). A *salumeria* will specialise more in smoked meats, whereas an *alimentario* will also have things like baby food and cakes. There will be shelves of tinned food like artichokes (*carciofi*), asparagus (*asparagi*), sweet peppers (*peperoni*), canned seafood like mussels (*cozze*) and clams, and the counter will have a row of barrels containing olives and anchovies with strings of salami and cured ham hanging from the ceiling.

Italy has one of the largest selections of cured meats in Europe. Parma ham is the best known internationally. Sliced extra thin a little goes a long way in sandwiches or served for supper with melon or fresh figs. Other cured ham (*prosciutto crudo*) will be produced locally and is slightly cheaper. *Bresaola* is air-dried beef also served in wafer thin slices, usually with a little oil dribbled over and seasoned with black pepper.

Cheaper meats include *mortadella*, which is an enormous plump sausage shape and is studded with pork fat and sometimes pistachio nuts, and all kinds of salami, the best and most expensive of which is called *coppa*. Again, different regions will have their local specialities of salami and most shops will give you a little piece to try first. *Panchetta* is a salted streaky bacon good eaten raw in sandwiches. Two kinds of sausages that need to be cooked are *luganega* and *cotechino*.

Butter, which is usually unsalted, is quite expensive, sometimes double the cost in Britain. Yoghurts are usually locally made and very good. Cream is more popular here than further south, but not as widely used as in England.

Cheese (*formaggio*)

There is a big variety of cheeses in Italy, even in the mountains. You will find nationally known types like the hard *Parmesan* (used grated in cooking and for sprinkling on pasta dishes), and *mozzarella* which is used in pizzas to make that lovely gooey stringy effect as well as eaten uncooked in salads, particularly with tomatoes and fresh basil. *Mozzarella* made from cow's milk is available everywhere and should be eaten as fresh as possible, as should *ricotta*, a soft white cheese which gives a creamy result in cooked dishes and is very easy to digest.

Blue cheeses like Gorgonzola and Castelmagno are for those who like strong flavours — not recommended for packing in your suitcase to take home! Keep them covered to

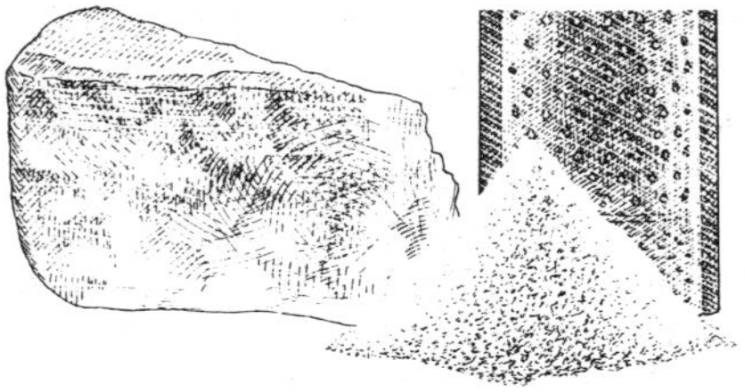

Parmesan cheese

limit the smell and also preserve the flavour. Bel Paese is a processed cheese which comes in individual portions, popular with children and good for taking in your pocket for a mid-morning snack on the slopes.

So much for the better known varieties. In the mountains you will find lots of cheeses marked *nostrano* which means local and the only thing to do is experiment. The Aosta Valley, for example, has some excellent local kinds like *fontina valdostana*, which is pale with a russet rind. The word *fontina* is stamped on the rind and its creamy texture makes it ideal for sprinkling grated on soups and pasta as well as making into the local variety of *fondue*. (La Maison de Fromage in Courmayeur is a typical example of a local cheese shop and it even stocks tins of *fontina* ready-prepared as a *fondue* sauce.)

Tome is another mountain cheese, with a mild flavour. It is easy to digest and is especially suitable for children.

GREENGROCERS (*fruttivendolo*)

Althought the supply of fresh produce is naturally more limited in the winter months, you will always be able to find apples (*mela*), oranges (*arancia*) and usually pears (*pera*). Mandarins and oranges are brought up to the mountains from the south. In Italy, potatoes (*patata*) are treated with the respect they deserve (you will find a number of local dishes based around the potato in restaurants), and onions (*cipolle*) and celery (*sedano*) are widely available. Look out for Jerusalem artichokes (*topinambur*), which resemble potatoes but are slightly knobbly; they are excellent sautéd in butter. In spring you will find spinach (*spinaci*) is good value, and it is worth trying chard (*biete*), which looks like spinach with thick white stems.

If your resort is not too remote you will find a good variety of lettuces (*lattuga*), including *radicchio* (which is in fact related to the cabbage) with a tight head of purple leaves which have a bitter taste – excellent mixed with the mild lambs' tongue lettuce (*pasqualina*). Sweet peppers (*peperoni*) and aubergines (*melanzane*) can be cooked together to make a ratatouille with garlic (*aglio*), which you will see everywhere. Prices for the more expensive items both in greengrocers and in some other food shops may be marked by the 100g (3½oz) instead of the kilo.

BUTCHERS (*macelleria*)

You will find in many towns that chicken (*pollo*) and eggs (*uova*) are sold in a shop called a *polleria*. Local chickens will generally be corn-fed and very tasty; supermarket varieties are more factory-farmed like their British equivalent. There are also various different kinds of chicken you can buy depending on the dish you are making, older ones being more suitable for soups. Chicken pieces are available too; useful if all your kitchen contains is one blunt knife.

Winter sees a good selection of game – pheasant (*fagiano*), partridge (*pernici*), quail (*quaglie*), venison (*cervo*) and rabbit (*coniglio*) are available most of the time. Veal (*vitello*) is an Italian speciality, and can be bought in escalopes, chops or breast. It is not cheap, but generally of good quality. Beef (*manzo*) is variable and best made into stews, unless you ask for fillet (*filetto*) or sirloin (*contra filleto*); other cuts sold as 'steak', on or off the bone, can be pretty tough. The butcher will mince it for you if asked. Baby lamb (*abbachio*) is available in spring but older lamb (*agnello*) is not as common as in Britain. For cheaper meals try frying some liver (*fegato*) with herbs.

BAKERY (*panettiere, panificio, fornaio*)

There is a large variety of bread in Italy, and each region has its speciality. Croissants are good for breakfast, while sliced bread is available (mostly from supermarkets) for toast, should your apartment have a grill or toaster. Wholemeal bread (*pane integral*) is sold alongside lots of different sorts of white – round, sticks, rolls and so on. You will find a good selection of biscuits and cakes for tea, many made of nuts and fruit, like *amaretti*, which are macaroons containing almonds, or *panettone*, a large dome-shaped cake with sultanas and candied peel.

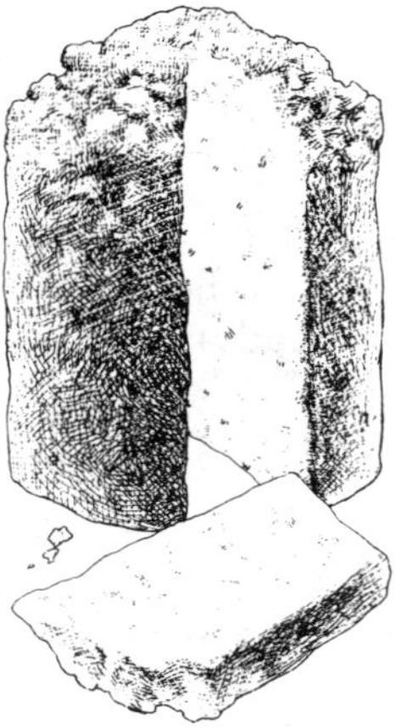

Panettone

9

ITALIAN WINE

Few people realise that Italy is the world's largest wine producer. Unlike France or Germany, Italy until fairly recently had no regulations governing its wine production; thus it was harder for the country to gain an international reputation, since standards were so erratic. Until the end of the 1950s, wine drinking in Italy was largely a regional matter, with no analytical comparison of growths or vintages possible. However, in 1963, the government introduced the labelling system of Denominazioni di Origine Controllata, the now familiar DOC.

Once you have understood the DOC system, you can buy wine while on holiday that is either from that region or another, quite confidently. DOC not only stipulates the region of origin, but also regulates from what grapes and in what quantity certain wines can be made, as well as setting down minimum ageing periods for certain varieties. It is similar to the *appellation contrôlée* system used in France and can be taken as a guarantee of the authenticity of each bottle's background.

Wine in Italy is cheap by British standards, so it is definitely worth trying some of the DOC ones if you want to experience the best the country has to offer. Below I give some of the most common ones you are likely to find in the Alpine regions, as well as those best known in Britain which will be brought in from other regions. However, do experiment with the local *vini di tavola* (table wine) as well. Some are very pleasant indeed and almost cheaper than soft drinks!

You may remember that during the recent Austrian wine

scandal, when it was discovered anti-freeze had been added to increase sweetness, that Italy underwent a similar upset when it came to light that certain producers had also been adulterating their wine. The Italian government reacted with swiftness and severity, immediately introducing a random testing system and a seal which guaranteed bottles from a tested and cleared batch. Consequently the Italian wine trade has recovered quickly from this setback, and you can enjoy the enormous variety it offers its domestic as well as its export market with no anxieties.

Piedmont

A fertile region bordering France and Switzerland, Piedmont boasts some of the best Italian wines. Those who go skiing in resorts like Macugnaga, Sestriere, Sauze D'Oulx and Claviere can buy top quality wines which have travelled no further than a few kilometres up the valley. However, their high standard means they are available in most other resorts as well.

The best is without doubt Barolo, a full-bodied red called the 'king of wine and wine of kings'. With its slightly gentler stablemate Barbaresco, it has recently been promoted to the highest section of the DOC wines, called DOCG. The taste improves with age, so look out for those from the 1978 and 1974 vintages. Two other reds which come close to Barolo for their high standard are Gattinara and Spanna, but you need to buy the right vintage to taste the best of them – ask the wine shop for advice. Carema, grown at 760m (2,500ft) near the Aosta Valley, Grignolino, Ghemme, Sizzano and Nebbiolo d'Alba are other DOC wines to look out for.

There are fewer whites produced, the most notable being Cortese di Gavi (sometimes known just as Gavi), a fragrant and delicate wine of which a sparkling variety is also available. The most famous sparkling wine is of course Asti Spumante. Personally I find it too sweet and not a patch on the French dry sparkling wines, but it is all a matter of personal taste and if you fancy having a 'champagne' breakfast, this is a good cheap way of doing it!

Aosta Valley

Until fairly recently French was the main language in this region, although it was clamped down on during the fervent nationalism of the Mussolini era. Italian is now taught and spoken everywhere, but you will find that many wine and food labels as well as signs and shop names are still in French.

Very little wine from the Aosta Valley is imported to Britain, so if you're skiing in Courmayeur or Cervinia, make the most of your chance to try some. There are only a very few DOC wines of which Donnaz and Enfer D'Arvier are the most notable (now incorporated under the Valle D'Aosta umbrella denomination). Two very good whites are Blanc de Morgex and Blanc de La Salle, which go well with the river trout and cheese *fondues* served in the local restaurants. The non-DOC wines are reliably delicate and refreshing, and quite often have a slight sparkle, without being actually fizzy.

Lombardy

Those skiers who fly to Milan and then continue by coach up past the lakes to resorts like Livigno (which is a duty-free zone), Madesimo, Bormio and Chiesa will be familiar with the sight of fertile plains giving rise to terraced vineyards. Lombardy is a very productive area in agriculture as well as its industry which is centred around Milan. The best-known wine is made from grapes grown on the steep terraces of Valtellina, near the Swiss border. Valtellina are excellent red wines, the most superior of which are the velvety Sassella, Grumello, Valgella and Inferno. Sfursat is made from grapes that have been partly dried and this is a wine worth taking home to mature.

From southern Lombardy come the Oltrepo Pavese wines, which rank between the best and the everyday, both red and white. Near Brescia, which is a centre for food products as well as wine, Botticino is produced. If you want a sparkling wine made by the champagne method try Franciacorta, also available as still red and white wine. A good white from the Lake Garda area is Lugana, fruity and soft without being sweet.

Trentino-Alto Adige

These two areas lie south of the Austrian border and take much from their northern neighbour in both food and wine. In the Alto Adige part, closest to Austria, the wines often have Germanic-looking labels and certainly taste closer to those from northern climes, like Alsace, than from sunny Italy. Try the reds like Caldaro and Santa Maddalena, the pale white Terlano from Bolzano or the red Meranese from Merano. These wines are widely available in ski resorts like Selva and Cortina, which lie in the beautiful range of mountains called the Dolomites just to the east.

10

REGIONAL DISHES IN THE ITALIAN ALPS

Italy is still a country of strongly defined regions and nowhere is this more true than its diversity of cuisine. Local dishes can differ widely from valley to valley and be totally unfamiliar to people living 150 or so kilometres away, something almost unthinkable in England. This is particularly true in the mountainous regions, where until recently each valley was very much a self-contained unit, locked in by snow in winter. Modern communications and the increase in travelling by Italians and tourists does mean of course that certain dishes and ingredients can be seen throughout Italy, but you will still generally find that the local variety is cheaper and, if eaten in a restaurant, better cooked.

RECIPES

Those dishes marked with an asterisk could be made while you are in the area. The others, being more complicated or requiring special equipment, are best left till you get home to try out. In the meantime, enjoy them in the local restaurants.

Zuppa pavese (broth with egg)*
Minestrone*
Bagna cauda (hot dip)
Fonduta (cheese *fondue*)
Risotto alla Milanese (simple risotto)*
Polenta (cooked corn meal)

Peperoni alla Piedmontese (Piedmontese stuffed peppers)*
Osso buco (braised shin of veal)
Vitello valdostana (Aosta Valley veal escalopes)*
Zabaglione*
Monte Bianco pudding

Broth with egg
(zuppa pavese)

For those who want a quick soup, *zuppa pavese* fits the bill nicely. It is served in virtually every restaurant in Italy, but the claims to its origins lie in Lombardy. Serves 4

1¼ litres (2¼ pints) good chicken broth
12 small slices bread (taken from a bread stick)
4 eggs
butter or butter and oil for frying
4 tablespoons grated Parmesan

Put the broth into a large saucepan to come to the boil. Fry the bread in butter or a mixture of butter and oil. Break each egg into a cup, and then slip it into the boiling broth to poach. After about 4 minutes, lift an egg into the bottom of each soup bowl (it will almost certainly break which doesn't really matter), pour the broth over, arrange the bread on top and sprinkle with the grated cheese. Serve immediately.

Minestrone

In Britain the best known of Italian soups is undoubtedly minestrone and there are dozens of different ways of making it. Simply use a little of any vegetables that you have around, being sure to include a bit of gammon or bacon, some small pasta shapes, some kind of white bean and preferably some tomatoes. The rest is up to you, but here is a suggestion. Serves 4–6

2 tablespoons olive oil
1 large onion
1 large clove garlic
100g (3½oz) piece gammon or bacon
450g (1lb) fresh or 400g (14oz) tin tomatoes
1 tablespoon tomato purée
2 courgettes
100g (3½oz) French beans
400g (14oz) tin white haricot beans
handful small pasta shapes or broken up spaghetti
salt and black pepper
1 celery stick

800 ml-1¼ litres (1½-2¼ pints) chicken stock
bay leaf
2 tablespoons grated Parmesan cheese
2 tablespoons chopped parsley

Slice the onion, gammon, celery, courgettes and French beans. Heat the oil in a saucepan, add the onion, garlic and gammon and fry for 5 minutes. Stir in the tomato purée and tomatoes (chopped if using fresh), the chicken stock, bay leaf and celery. Cover and simmer for 40 minutes.

Add the remaining vegetables, haricot beans and pasta and simmer a further 10–15 minutes. Sprinkle with the parsley, season well and serve with grated Parmesan cheese.

Hot dip
(*bagna cauda*)

This pungent heated sauce from Piedmont is served in an earthenware dish over a small spirit lamp as a 'snack' with raw vegetables to dip into it. (Cook it in an earthenware dish if you have one which is flameproof, otherwise a saucepan is fine.) For lovers of garlic it is superb, but you should be warned it is pretty indigestible. A fairly rough local wine will cut through the tastes.

5 cloves garlic
150-300 ml (¼-½ pint) olive oil
175-225 g (6-8 oz) anchovy fillets
3-4 tablespoons butter
pepper
selection of available raw vegetables, cut into batons

Melt the butter in a saucepan, cook the crushed garlic until it starts to brown, stir in the chopped anchovies and oil and freshly ground pepper. Cook for 10 minutes, stirring, until the anchovies have disintegrated. Serve immediately, with batons of raw green and red peppers, celery, carrots and so on, to dip in the sauce.

Cheese fondue
(*fonduta*)

You need to bring back some of the *fontina* cheese from the Aosta Valley for an authentic version of this *fondue*, which is also popular in Piedmont, but Gruyère is an acceptable substitute. The combination of the truffles and cheese gives a subtle flavour and you'd do best to buy the truffles out there too. An excellent dish to eat while in the area – you will find that many restaurants serve it. Serves 6

500g (1¼lb) fontina *cheese*
6 eggs
about 450ml (¾ pint) milk
1 tablespoon butter
seasoning
2-3 white truffles
cubed bread for dipping

Cut the rind off the cheese, then dice it into small pieces and cover with the milk for about 3–4 hours. Beat the eggs and put them in a saucepan with the cheese and milk, season well. Cook very gently, stirring all the time. When the ingredients become thick and gooey, pour into an earthenware casserole and cover the surface with sliced truffle. Keep the casserole hot by placing it over a spirit lamp. Dip pieces of cubed bread into the *fonduta* to scoop it up.

Simple risotto
(risotto alla Milanese)

This classic rice dish uses a few simple ingredients, which carefully cooked make a lovely creamy mixture to accompany dishes like *osso buco* or to eat alone as a starter or main course. With good risotto rice the end result should be smooth and creamy, but not sludgy. Serves 4

350g (12oz) risotto rice
2 tablespoons butter
1 small onion
200ml (7fl oz) white wine
pinch saffron
about 1¼ litres (2¼ pints) chicken stock
3 tablespoons grated Parmesan

Melt half the butter in a thick-bottomed frying pan, chop the onion finely and fry it gently in the butter until it starts to soften. Add the rice and stir to coat it well with the butter, then pour on the white wine and cook until it has almost bubbled away. Heat the stock in a separate saucepan and add it a cup at a time, waiting till it is almost absorbed before adding the next lot. The stock must be poured in boiling hot or it will halt the cooking of the dish and make the end result soggy. Stir from time to time, especially towards the end.

After about 20–25 minutes the rice should be almost cooked. Crush the saffron stamens and pour a cup of the stock over them, add to the risotto and stir until the colour has spread through and the stock cooked away. Stir in the rest of the butter and the cheese and serve.

Cooked corn meal
(*polenta*)

This yellow maize flour (or corn meal) is one of the staple foods of northern Italy, and although you may think it rather bland if served in a classy restaurant further south, after a morning's skiing in the mountains it will be a very welcome filling dish to accompany your lunch.

It is traditionally made by bringing a large deep pan containing about 1½ litres (2½ pints) of water to the boil, adding about 450g (1lb) of finely ground polenta and leaving over a gentle fire to cook for an hour, stirring often with a long wooden stick. The dish is then upended over a wooden board (the water having been absorbed) and the *polenta* comes out as a solid cake, in the shape of the rounded base of the pan.

It can be eaten plain in place of bread, or mixed with cream, meat sauces, cheese, sautéd mushrooms and truffles and other ingredients which transform it into a more tasty dish.

Piedmontese stuffed peppers
(peperoni alla Piedmontese)

These are served locally as an *antipasto* (hors d'oeuvre), but if accompanied by other substantial salads they can in fact make a good, meatless main course. Using different coloured peppers gives an attractive look to the dish. Serves 6

6 sweet peppers
2-3 cloves garlic
3 tomatoes
6 anchovy fillets
2 tablespoons olive oil
seasoning
55g (2oz) butter
1 tablespoon fresh chopped parsley
vinaigrette

Halve the peppers lengthways and remove all the central core, seeds and so on. Large ones can be halved again. Peel the tomatoes, first dipping them in boiling water to loosen the skins, halve them, remove the pips and then chop roughly. Chop the anchovy fillets. Mix the tomatoes with the anchovy, crushed garlic and olive oil, season lightly and pile onto the sweet peppers.

Dot the tops with butter and bake. Bake in a preheated medium oven for 30 minutes, then cool, sprinkle with parsley and serve with a vinaigrette. The peppers should still have some bite to them.

Braised shin of veal
(osso buco)

Winter calls for warming stews, and none is better than this one made from sawn up veal shin. It needs to be cooked at a slow simmer until the meat is so tender it is virtually falling off the bone. Serves 4

1kg (2¼lb) shin of veal, sawn into 6-8cm (2½-3in) pieces with marrow intact
seasoning
flour for dredging the meat
2 tablespoons butter
2 tablespoons olive oil
1 onion
1-2 cloves garlic
450g (1lb) fresh tomatoes or 400g (14oz) can
150-300ml (¼-½ pint) white wine
a little hot stock

Garnish
1 clove garlic, grated rind of 1 lemon, 1 tablespoon chopped parsley

Sprinkle the veal pieces with salt and black pepper and roll them in the flour. Heat the oil and butter in a large broad-bottomed casserole and brown the meat. Remove it, slice the onion and sauté it with the crushed garlic until soft but not brown.

Replace the veal in the casserole, standing each piece upright or the succulent marrow will slither out in the cooking. Add the tomatoes (peeled, seeded and chopped if fresh) and wine, and a little hot stock so the liquid comes just to the top of the veal pieces. Bring to the boil and simmer very gently for 1½–2 hours depending on the size of the bones. The meat should end up so tender it is virtually falling off the bone.

To garnish, mix the finely chopped garlic with the grated lemon rind and chopped parsley and sprinkle over the dish immediately before serving. Traditionally served with *risotto alla Milanese* (see above).

Aosta Valley veal escalopes *(vitello Valdostana)*

These are veal escalopes or thin chops, covered in ham and melted cheese, from the Aosta Valley. Recipes vary from one restaurant to another; the end result is pretty filling! Note that this is made with plain cooked ham, not the cured *prosciutto* variety. Serves 4

4 veal escalopes
175-225g (6-8oz) fontina *cheese (mozzarella will do)*
4 large slices cooked ham
55g (2oz) butter
seasoning
fresh basil

Melt the butter in a frying pan and quickly fry the veal on both sides until cooked. Cool slightly while you chop the basil. Remove the escalopes and sprinkle with the chopped basil and seasoning. Wrap each one in a slice of ham, place in a heatproof serving dish and sprinkle liberally with the cheese. Place under a hot grill or in a hot oven until the cheese is melted and bubbling and the meat has heated right through.

Zabaglione

After a heavy meal this slips down very easily. It should be as fluffy as possible, but take care it doesn't curdle while cooking. Serves 4

4 egg yolks
4 tablespoons Marsala wine
50g (2oz) caster sugar

Lightly mix the egg yolks with the wine and sugar in a pudding basin. Place this over a small pan of just simmering water and whisk continuously until thick and fluffy. This will take about 5 minutes or a little longer. Pour the mixture into tall glasses, previously warmed, and serve immediately.

Monte Bianco pudding

Although Mont Blanc (Monte Bianco in Italian) actually lies just in France, it is on the Italian side that you are more likely to find this famous dessert. Do not be fooled by the simplicity of its ingredients; chestnuts are rich and filling, and when they are combined with the cream you will find it hard afterwards to rise from the table! Serves 4-6

700g ($1\frac{1}{2}$lb) unpeeled chestnuts
125g (4oz) caster sugar
pinch salt
150ml ($\frac{1}{4}$ pint) double cream

Drop the chestnuts into boiling water in small batches and simmer for 10 minutes, then remove them and, wearing rubber gloves to protect your hands, peel the outer and inner skins off with a small knife while still hot. Have the next batch in the water while you peel the previous ones.

Boil up some fresh water and then simmer the chestnuts for 45–60 minutes until really tender. Drain and mash with the sugar and a large pinch of salt. Then press the chestnuts through a strong sieve, a food mill, or ideally an old-fashioned potato ricer (looks like a huge garlic press), straight onto the serving dish. The chestnut will come out in little light worm-shapes and fall naturally into a peak shape.

Whip the cream not too stiffly and gently spread it over the 'mountain' of chestnut. Don't press down or you will crush out the light airy texture of the pudding. Chill for about 30 minutes and serve. This is best made not too far ahead of serving.

AUSTRIA

11

SHOPPING IN THE AUSTRIAN ALPS

Austria is the most popular destination for British skiers, with more than half of us who decide on a winter sports holiday choosing one of its friendly resorts. However, the number of self-catering apartments is smaller than these numbers would lead us to believe, with most accomodation being in family-run pensions and small hotels. One popular arrangement is studio apartments attached to hotels, where you can use the kitchenette to prepare meals and snacks, but also have the option of eating in the hotel restaurant. Unlike the purpose-built apartment blocks in the French Alps, here in Austria they are often tucked away in ordinary houses, cleverly converted.

The variety of resorts and facilities makes it hard to generalise about what is available in the shops. I have indicated below what you will always find, but have given an idea too on what is on sale in the larger, more sophisticated resorts like Lech. Wherever you go you will find the shopkeepers almost invariably friendly and helpful.

SUPERMARKET AND GROCER (*Supermarkt und Lebensmittelgeschäft*)

Even the smallest village will have a general store; in the bigger resorts you will find a supermarket, often brand new. The one-stop general store sells everything from butter

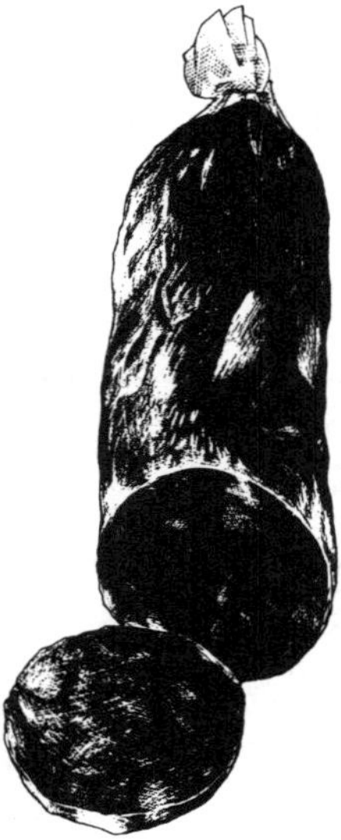

Sausage

(*Butter*) to sugar (*Zucker*), including meat (*Fleisch*). The larger villages have more specialised shops with, for instance, a separate butcher and so on. A wide range of tinned goods is available, including tinned soups and casseroles, vegetables like sauerkraut and red cabbage, as well as packet soups, stock cubes, tubes of tomato purée and all the dried herbs and spices you need.

The delicatessen counter will, even in small places, have an excellent range of smoked hams (*Schinken*) and sausages (*Wurste*). Many of these are made locally, but it is often necessary to import them too to cope with demand during the season. Small sausages like frankfurters and *Burenwurst* are good for easy suppers and in salads, larger one like *Krakauer* and *Dürre* are sliced for you on the premises and make excellent sandwich fillings. Don't miss *Tiroler Bauernspeck*, a piquant, home-cured bacon, served raw in a chunk or ready-sliced. You can find beef as well as pork smoked sausages.

For picnic lunches you can buy rolls filled with the ingredients of your choice at these delicatessen counters, which saves a lot of time and effort. You will find the choice is mainly between cheeses and smoked meats — the kinds of ready-mixed salads we are familiar with in our supermarkets are not so common. The freezer cabinet will offer a variety of ready-cooked meals, frozen fish, and some raw meat like pork chops and chicken.

Yoghurt is sold nearly everywhere, as well as *crème fraîche*, which is a slightly sour cream-yoghurt, very good for cooking. In the bigger stores you will find English tea, Nuttella spread, cornflakes and other more luxury items. You can get eggs here too, but in many areas you can buy them straight from the local farms, although the farmers rarely speak English.

There is a large selection of cheese (*Käse*). The Austrian ones tend to be quite hard, sometimes almost rubbery. These are either processed or natural, and often smoked. Varieties include Emmental in wheels or blocks (processed, natural or smoked), Edam, Gouda, Tilsiter and Gruyère. You will also find the softer, creamier French-style camemberts. It is not uncommon to eat cheese and sliced *Wurst* for breakfast with rolls. Try Graukas, a greyish kind of cottage cheese left in a warm place and covered, either eaten as it is, or with salt and pepper and onions on bread.

Meat and fish (*Fleisch und Fisch*)

Meat in Austria is expensive, up to twice the price it is in England. Pork (*Schweinefleisch*), mince (*Gehachte*) and veal (*Kalbfleisch*) escalopes for *Wiener Schnitzel* are popular, beef (*Rindfleisch*) is very pricey (so steaks as a quick supper might not be such a bright idea), chicken (*Huhn/Hendl*) costs only a little more than here.

The only fresh fish available is trout (*Forelle*). Frozen fish from supermarket cabinets includes cod in batter, prawns (*Garnelen*) and so on. Smoked trout is a local delicacy.

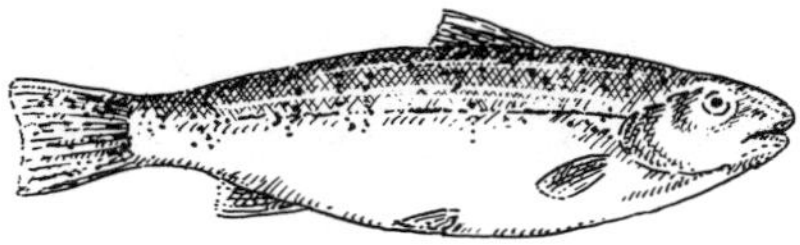

Trout

Fruit and vegetables (*Obst und Gemüse*)

The choice of vegetables varies considerably from one resort to another. You will always find potatoes (*Kartoffeln*), onions (*Zwiebeln*), cauliflower (*Blumenkohl*) and cabbage — but only the white (*Kohl*) or red (*Rotkohl*) varieties. Kohlrabi is

Green and red peppers

popular in Austria, a kind of turnip-shaped vegetable it can be cooked in chunks or grated in salads. There should be a good selection of salad stuffs like *radicchio*, red and green peppers (*Ziegenpfeffer*), tomatoes (*Tomaten*) and so on. French beans (*grüne Bohnen*) are sold too. All these are usually much cheaper than in England.

In big resorts like Lech there is an excellent selection of imported vegetables like broccoli (*Spargelkohl*), asparagus (*Spargel*), courgettes (*Zucchini*), fennel (*Fenchel*) and so on. Anything brought in will obviously be more expensive. In late autumn you can buy the cabbage speciality sauerkraut (pickled white cabbage) freshly made in little tubs, the rest of the year it is tinned or in sealed packets.

With fruit, again, the choice varies enormously. Apples (*Apfeln*), bananas (*Bananen*) and oranges (*Orangen*) are commonplace; in some resorts you will find pineapples (*Ananas*), grapes (*Trauben*), along with kiwi fruit (*Kiwi Frucht*), apricots (*Marillen*), plums (*Pflaumen*), even strawberries (*Erdbeeren*) and peaches (*Pfirsche*). The quality of all these is generally high.

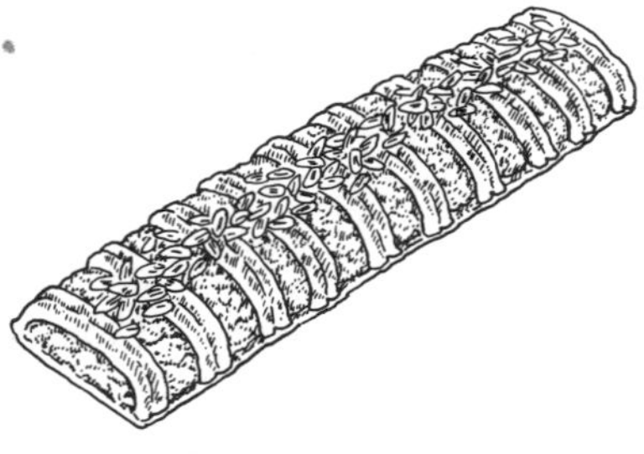

Strudel

BAKERY (*Bäckerei*)

There is a very good variety of bread in Austria, made from wheat, rye, or a mixture of grains. You can either get big country loaves, similar to our granary bread, or little rolls (*Semmel*) and plaits of white bread, generally the harder-crusted sort. The village baker will often deliver. There is also an enormous selection of cakes and flans (*Kuchen und Torten*), often covered with whipped cream (*Schlagsahne*), as well as strudels.

Finally, Austria makes some excellent chocolates, and I would particularly recommend the Mozart ones by Mirabell of Salzburg.

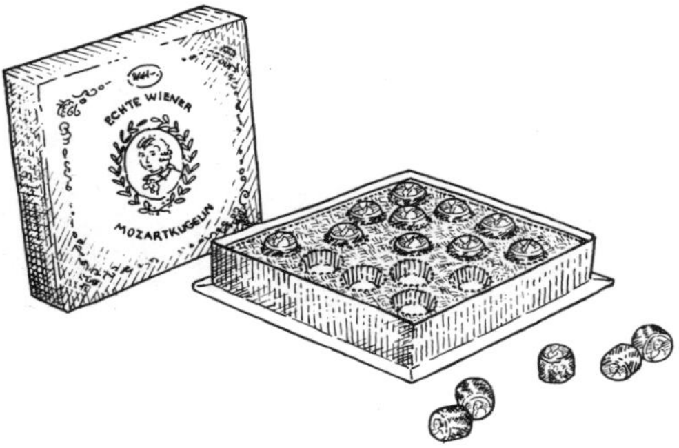

Chocolates

12

AUSTRIAN WINE

Unlike Italy, where good quality wine is often produced just a few kilometres down the valley from your ski resort, the Austrian Alps import most of their best wines from the vineyards in the eastern part of the country. Perfectly drinkable everyday local wine is produced as well, most notably in South Tirol, which has some quite good reds, but for the better quality wine you should look out for the labels below.

Austrian wine is rarely exported, with most of the yield going to make pleasant light table wines, 85 per cent of them white and often with a slight sparkle. The standard of this *Tafelwein* is high and you will find dozens of different varieties to try. Local wine is often served on draught when it is known as *Offenerwein* (open wine).

Austria's wine reputation was dealt an enormous blow due to the wine scandal of 1985, but new Austrian Wine Laws now guarantee the strictest standards and purity. The best bottles of wine come from the following regions:

Lower Austria Despite its name, which would make you think this area lies in southern Austria, it is in fact in the north-east. The principal vineyards are in the Wachau district in the Danube valley near Krems. From here come a lot of Riesling type wines, including a delicate white called Kremser, Dürsteiner, and Brünnerstrassler, which has a slight sparkle. Grinzig is another sparkling one. The more expensive Schloss Grafenegg from Prince Metternich's estate, bottled in his Krems cellars, also has a good reputation.

Slightly to the north-east of the Krems/Wachau area,

running up to the Czech border, is the Weinviertel district. Here some light reds are produced from Retz, Pulkau, Poysdorf, Matzen and Falkenstein.

Burgenland Wines from this part of Austria, which lies just south-east of Vienna, have a great reputation. Ones worth looking out for are the golden white Ruster wines, including the Tokay dessert variety, Gumpoldskirchen, another sweet white which is quite strong, Nussberger and the reds from Vöslauer and Rust. Blaufrankisch is a good red to try.

Styria On the Yugoslav border the vineyards of Styria produce Traminer, one of the best Austrian whites, as well as some light reds.

OTHER DRINKS

Austrian beer, available bottled and on draught, tastes light and refreshing but is in fact quite strong — try the Tyrolean Zillertaler. Pilsner Urquell, a Czech beer, is also widely available, while Schlossgold and Kronenthaler are brands of non-alcoholic beer. Spirits include the famous schnapps made from local fruits like *Slivowitz* (plum) and *Enzian* (from gentian flowers which give it a slightly bitter taste), as well as liqueurs and brandies made from apricots, pears, cherries and raspberries. Most bottles have a picture on the label indicating which fruit the contents are based on, which does away with any language problem!

Mineral waters from Austrian spas are inexpensive and widely available, and the sparkling ones are often mixed with the excellent local apple juice (ask for *einer gesplitzte Apfelsaft*). Pure grape juice (*Traubensaft*) is also very good, if a little sweet for some tastes. Imported gin and whisky are expensive.

13

REGIONAL DISHES IN THE AUSTRIAN ALPS

All but a few of Austria's ski resorts are in the three western provinces: Land Salzburg, Vorarlberg and Tirol (Tyrol). Before tourism arrived, these mountain villages consisted of fairly isolated settlements of farmers and herders, where it was rare to travel far from the local valley. The cuisine reflects this peasant background, especially in Tirol and Vorarlberg, which until recently remained little influenced by developments in the cities. When eating out you will find the local dishes are simple rustic fare, usually served in enormous portions, which may defeat even the heartiest appetite.

Traditionally, the main meal is served at lunchtime, with a cold supper of meats and salad, and perhaps a bowl of soup in the evening, but obviously in resorts where customers are out skiing all day, the pattern is more flexible. Here the 12 till 2pm lunch hour is extended and it is not uncommon to see notices outside the local *Gasthof* or inn advertising *Ganztägig warme Küche* (hot meals all day long). On the slopes themselves, head for the *Jausenstatione* (snack stations) where you can enjoy an open sandwich or a filling dish of *G'Röstl* or dumpling soup.

RECIPES

Those dishes marked with an asterisk could be made while you are in the area. The others, being more complicated or requiring special equipment, are best left till you get home to try out. In the meantime, enjoy them in the local restaurants.

Gulaschsuppe (goulash soup)*
Graupensuppe (barley soup)*
Schlick Krapfen (dumplings with ham)
Nockerl (fried dumplings)
Spätzle (dumplings)
Wiener Schnitzel (breaded veal escalopes)*
G'Röstl (meat and potato hash)*
Zillertaler Krapfen (turnovers)
Tiroler Leber (Tyrolean liver)*
Salzburger Nockerl (sweet soufflé)
Doboz Torte (caramel cake)

Throughout the Austrian Alps you will find some pretty substantial soups, which are almost a meal in themselves. Bean soup (*Bohnensuppe*), dumpling soup and goulash soup are but three.

Goulash soup
(Gulaschsuppe)

Serves 6

200g (7oz) braising beef
1 frankfurter sausage
3 large onions
2 sticks celery
3 tablespoons oil
pinch salt
pinch caraway seeds
1 teaspoon paprika
dash vinegar
1 tablespoon tomato purée
1½ litres (2½ pints) water
3 large potatoes

Dice the beef finely, slice the frankfurter. Slice the onion and celery finely and fry them in the hot oil until golden brown, then add the salt, spices and vinegar. Stir, put in the beef and tomato purée and stir until the meat is browned. Add the sliced frankfurter, pour in the water, bring to the boil, cover and simmer for 20 minutes. Peel and dice the potatoes, add them, with a little more water if necessary, and simmer for a further 15–20 minutes until soft.

Barley Soup
(Graupensuppe)

In Austria, as in Switzerland, barley can be grown at quite high altitudes and a variety of barley soups find their way on to local menus. This broth is a lighter way of making it, using a vegetable stock and no meat. It is therefore more suitable as a first course than a main meal. Serves 6

125g (4oz) pearl barley
1 medium onion
1 stick celery
1½ litres (2½ pints) good vegetable stock (or water and 2-3 vegetable stock cubes)
3 tablespoons butter
1 tablespoon flour
seasoning
bay leaf
3 tablespoons thick cream
2 tablespoons fresh chopped parsley

Finely chop the celery and onion and gently fry them in the butter with the barley. Stir in the flour to absorb the fat and add the stock, stirring all the time, then season well and add the bay leaf. Bring to the boil and simmer, covered, for about an hour.

Stir in the cream, and serve. A little chopped parsley in each bowl livens up the pale appearance of this nourishing broth.

Dumplings are a staple part of Austrian mountain cooking, although the recipes and textures differ considerably from region to region. The common name is *Knödel*, which covers either large or smaller dumplings, the latter dropped into soups towards the end of the cooking time to absorb the flavours. *Nockerl* are small to medium sized 'dumplings', halfway between a *soufflé* and Italian *gnocchi*.

Dumplings with ham
(Schlick Krapfen)

Little dumplings stuffed with a variety of savoury fillings are a delicious way of turning a simple clear broth into a fairly substantial dish. Serves 4–6

Dough
150g (5oz) plain flour
pinch salt
1 egg
1 tablespoon butter

Filling
175g (6oz) cooked meat or smoked ham, minced
2 tablespoons butter or dripping
1 small onion
1 tablespoon freshly chopped parsley or chopped spinach
pinch paprika
seasoning
1 egg, beaten

To cook
little flour
little milk

Sift the flour with the salt into a bowl, make a small depression in the centre and drop in the egg. Dice the butter and cut it into the flour and egg, then mix it all together and knead till smooth by hand. Set on one side.

Chop the onion finely and fry it in the fat until soft, then add the parsley and minced meat or ham. Season and add the paprika, remove from the heat and stir in the beaten egg.

On a floured board roll out the dough in long strips about 5cm (2½in) wide. Put small dabs of filling at intervals along one side of each strip, brush the uncovered paste with milk and fold it over the meat, pressing down to seal the join. Cut into individual squares and press the freshly cut joins to seal.

When all the pastry and filling is used up drop into the boiling broth to simmer gently for 15 minutes, before serving.

Fried dumplings
(Nockerl)

Lightly boiled and then fried gently in butter, these are served as an accompaniment to stews like *Gulasch*. Serves 6

250g (9oz) plain flour
1 tablespoon butter
300ml (½ pint) milk
1 egg
1 tablespoon butter for frying
salt
large pan of water

Sift the flour into a bowl. Heat half the butter and all the milk in a saucepan until blended, without boiling, then remove from the stove and whisk in the egg with a pinch of salt. Stir this mixture into the flour until you have a stiff paste. Bring a large pan of salted water to the boil, cut out the *Nockerl* with a small teaspoon and drop them into the boiling water to cook for 2 or 3 minutes. Drain, rinse under a cold tap and leave covered until needed.

To serve, heat the rest of the butter in a large frying pan and lightly sauté the *Nockerl* until heated through, shaking the pan to prevent them from browning.

Dumplings
(Spätzle)

These little dumplings from Vorarlberg look similar to the Tyrolean *Nockerln*, but are made from a much softer dough. They can be served plain instead of potatoes to accompany a meat dish, fried in a pan and served with sour cream (*Geröstete Spätzle*) or as a main course sprinkled with cheese and chives and accompanied by a green salad (*Käsespätzle*).

Wiener Schnitzl

These thin breaded escalopes of veal are of course originally named after Vienna (*Wien*), but they are now a staple part of every menu in Austria. Ask the butcher to beat the veal out for you. Serves 4

4 veal escalopes
flour
seasoning
1 large egg
dried beadcrumbs
2 tablespoons oil
75g (3oz) butter
2 lemons
1 tablespoon fresh chopped parsley

Cover a dinner plate with flour, season well and mix lightly. Beat the egg lightly on another plate and cover a third plate with the breadcrumbs. Line the plates up in that order. Lay both sides of the escalopes in the flour, knock off any excess then pass through the egg. Press down both sides in the breadcrumbs and set aside.

Heat the oil and 1oz (25g) butter in a frying pan and fry the escalopes for about 3 minutes each side until the breadcrumbs are golden brown. Remove and keep warm. Wipe out the pan, add the rest of the butter and cook until a nut-brown colour. Add the juice of one lemon, swirl around and pour over the escalopes. Serve sprinkled with the chopped parsley and garnished with lemon wedges.

Meat and potato hash
(G'Röstl)

This is a good cheap way of using up leftovers and is often seen on Tirolean restaurant menus. Exact quantities are not important, but make sure you season the dish well. Serves 4

2 tablespoons beef or pork dripping
2 cupfuls cooked potatoes
2 cupfuls cooked beef or pork
1 large onion
seasoning
caraway seeds
1-2 tablespoons freshly chopped parsley or chives

Slice the onion, dice the potatoes and cut the meat into shreds. Heat half the dripping in a heavy-bottomed frying pan and sauté the onion until golden brown. Lift out and set aside. Add the rest of the dripping and when hot add the potatoes to cook until brown, and then the meat. Take your time and allow these to become nicely browned and crisp before returning the onion with the seasoning and caraway seeds. Stir gently together until piping hot and serve sprinkled with the parsley.

If you wish you may slide a fried egg on top of each serving, which turns the dish into *Herrngröstl*. In either case it is good served with a salad of raw shredded savoy cabbage in a caraway seed dressing.

Turnovers
(Zillertaler Krapfen)

Those inns with a reputation for good food serve this dish as a weekend special. It's a cross between *ravioli* and *samosas* — little pastry turnovers filled with meat and deep fried in fat. Serves 4–6

Dough
225g (8oz) plain flour
pinch salt
1 egg
few tablespoons warm water
Filling
450g (1lb) potatoes
225g (8oz) low-fat cream cheese (Quark)
150ml (1/4pint) single cream or top of the milk
seasoning
1 egg yolk
1 dessertspoon flour
2-3 tablespoons freshly chopped parsley or chives
100g (3½oz) chopped ham

Sift the flour with the salt into a large bowl, make a well in the centre and drop in the egg. Stir slowly to draw in the flour and add enough warm water to make a stiff paste. Knead well by hand and set aside.

To make the filling, boil the potatoes, unpeeled, in salted water until done, then peel and sieve them while still hot. Beat in all the other filling ingredients with a dessertspoon or so of flour to make a firm paste.

Take the dough, knead lightly and shape into a long sausage. Cut into 2.5cm (1in) slices and roll each piece out as thinly as possible to form a circle. Drop a spoonful of filling in the centre of each round, brush round the edge with milk and fold over to form a semi-circular pasty. Press well to seal the edges and fry in really hot, deep fat.

Most menus in the Austrian Alps contain one or two dishes made of offal, testimony to the economical tradition of using up every part of the slaughtered animal. Those who like tripe should try *Beuschl*, where veal tripe is simmered until cooked and then served in a thick sour cream sauce with capers, mustard and anchovies, accompanied by dumplings – not something for those with light appetites! Liver is another popular dish.

Tirolean liver
(*Tiroler Leber*)

Serves 4

500g (1¼lb) calves' liver
little flour
2 tablespoons butter or dripping
1 small onion
seasoning
75ml (2½fl oz) stock
1 dessertspoon capers
1 dessertspoon vinegar
75ml (2½fl oz) sour cream or yoghurt

Slice the liver and roll it in a little flour, knock off any excess and fry in the hot fat until browned. Remove and set aside while you sauté the sliced onion until soft. Stir in a little flour to absorb the fat then blend in enough stock to make a thick sauce with the vinegar and chopped capers, seasoning well. Stir in the sour cream or yoghurt over a gentle heat (do not allow to boil or it will curdle).

Return the liver pieces and heat through for a few minutes then serve accompanied by *Nockerl*.

Sweet soufflé
(*Salzburger Nockerl*)

This is a more complicated relation of the straightforward *Nockerl*, eaten as a dessert. Here is one of many versions. Serves 4

6 eggs, separated
2 tablespoons icing sugar
2-3 tablespoons butter
3 tablespoons plain flour
little extra icing sugar

Set the oven at its top heat and put an ovenproof frying pan over a low heat on top of the stove.

Separate the eggs and beat the yolks till light. Whisk the whites and add the icing sugar to them, continuing to whisk well till smooth. Fold the egg yolks into the whites, then fold in the flour. Put the butter in the frying pan and, when it is foaming, put in six large spoonfuls of the egg mixture, piled up high and slightly separated in the pan.

When the undersides are cooked (about 30 seconds), put the frying pan into the oven and leave for a few minutes until the *Nockerl* have cooked through and are golden brown on top. Remove, sprinkle with a little more sugar and eat immediately before they collapse.

Caramel cake
(Doboz Torte)

Part of any holiday in Austria is indulging in the wickedly tempting array of cakes and pastries. Here is a recipe to recreate one of the simpler and less expensive ones. It is a little fiddly and time-consuming to make, but well worth the effort. Serves 6–8

Cake mixture
150g (5oz) plain flour
pinch salt
4 eggs
175g (6oz) caster sugar
Butter cream
55g (2oz) icing sugar
125g (4oz) butter (at room temperature
1 egg white
125g (4oz) plain chocolate
Caramel
150g (5oz) granulated sugar
150ml (1/4 pint) water
To finish
crushed caramel or grated plain chocolate

Take three large baking sheets, brush them with oil and dust with flour through a sieve. Mark two 20cm (8in) circles on each. Preheat the oven to Gas 5/375°F/190°C.

Sift the flour and salt. Break the eggs into a mixing bowl, add the sugar and beat with an electric whisk until thick and creamy light. Lightly fold in the flour, then divide into six and spread each portion over one of the circles on the trays. Bake for 5–6 minutes. Remove from the oven, trim round each circle to neaten it up and transfer to a wire rack to cool.

Make the butter cream by whisking the icing sugar and egg whites in a bowl over a pan of simmering water until it begins to hold its shape well. Cream the butter until really soft and gradually work the meringue mixture into it, a spoonful at a time. Melt the chocolate by placing it in a small bowl over a pan of simmering water and mix it into the butter cream.

Take five of the cake rounds and sandwich on top of each other with the butter cream. Make the caramel by melting the sugar in the water over a very low heat and then continue cooking over a high heat till you get a rich brown caramel. Immediately pour this over the sixth cake round on an oiled baking tray.

When the caramel has set, fix the final round on top of the others with more butter cream. Spread what's left around the outside of the cake and press on crushed caramel or grated chocolate.

SELF-CATERING RECIPES

14

INTRODUCTION

You are in the Alps to ski, not to cook. That doesn't mean you and your family or friends have to suffer hurried meals concocted entirely out of tins – to the contrary, getting together around the table at the end of the day and enjoying some good food can be one of the best parts of the holiday. Here are some tips on how to serve up good meals without wasting time:

Don't get bogged down in time-consuming dishes. If you follow the recipes in this section you will find that even if some take a while to cook, the preparation time rarely exceeds 15 minutes.

Only prepare one course. If your lot like more, serve pâté, cold meat, local smoked hams, cheese and fresh fruit.

Accompany the main course with the minimum of side dishes. Most of the casseroles here include plenty of vegetables, so all you'll need to cook as well are potatoes, rice or pasta. If you're having something a bit more fiddly, like fish, serve a big salad prepared in advance – you'll probably only have two rings in your kitchenette.

All recipes here indicate what can be prepared in the morning before you go out. If you can't face dealing with food in the morning, at least spend a little time checking you have all the ingredients for the evening meal and making a shopping list. The last thing you'll want to do when you stagger home is dash out to the shops for something you're lacking.

Don't become a martyr. Even if you have a reputation as the best cook in the party, rope in others to peel potatoes, lay the table, make salads or at least pour you a drink!

Plan a few meals at a time to cut down on shopping. For example, if you're cooking sausages, do double and have the rest cold in rolls for lunch the next day. Do extra rice or potatoes to use the leftovers in a salad.

KITCHEN TIPS

To crush garlic without a garlic crusher, peel it, cut into two or three, sprinkle with salt and squash with the blade of an ordinary table knife.

Marinading meat all day while you're out tenderises it as well as imparting delicious flavours.

Tubes of puréed garlic and herbs are excellent and convenient substitutes for the real thing.

Dried onion flakes can be useful for soups and stews; 3–4 tablespoons of flakes equals 1 medium onion.

It is worth taking with you a 15cm (6in) sharp kitchen knife (pack in your checked-in luggage if flying), a flat cheese grater and a packet of cornflour for thickening soups and casseroles.

15

PICNIC LUNCHES

Part of the fun of skiing in the Alps is enjoying the food served in the many mountainside restaurants scattered across the slopes. However, these become expensive if you use them every day, especially if you're paying for the whole family. In good weather there is nothing better than lying back against a snow bank and having a picnic. If you're skiing off-piste or doing cross-country skiing, it is often essential to take your own food.

Here are some tips for quick and easy lunches. The basic rule is keep it simple, use the local delicatessen, and make sure it can all be carried in your individual bum bag or little backpack. Wrap everything in silver foil or cling film.

Sandwich fillings

Using local rolls, bread or French sticks, you can quickly make up these sandwiches. Rye bread is a good variety to use for added taste. Remember to keep the butter out of the fridge overnight to soften it for spreading. A little salt and ground black pepper makes a world of difference to many sandwiches.

Tinned sardines, mashed with a fork, topped with sliced cucumber and chopped watercress.

Scrambled egg (cook extra at breakfast), topped with sliced tomato, chopped celery and mayonnaise.

Sliced hardboiled egg, salami (skin removed) and mayonnaise, with a little shredded lettuce.

Cream cheese, sliced bananas and a little honey.

BLT – crispy cooked bacon (rind removed), shredded lettuce and sliced tomato, with a little mayonnaise.

Tinned tuna fish mashed together with chopped celery, chopped cucumber and mayonnaise.

Cream cheese mixed with defrosted prawns, topped with shredded lettuce.

Avocado and cream cheese – scoop out the flesh of a ripe avocado, mash together with a tablespoon or two of cream cheese, seasoned with lemon juice and black pepper.

Don't forget to make use of the local pâtés, smoked meats, cheeses and fruit. My favourite sandwich for beating the cold and exhaustion is half a bar of plain dark chocolate in a soft white lightly buttered roll. Hardly healthy, but very cheering!

Remember, you may be falling over quite a bit. Don't take hardboiled eggs, glass bottles or anything else that will suffer or be dangerous if lain on.

16

SOUPS AND STARTERS

Skiing all day works up a healthy appetite, and what back home looks like enough food to feed four can be demolished by two in seconds on holiday in the Alps. Since food can be expensive there, especially in Switzerland, increasing the size of the main course or buying extra meat can knock your budget for six.

A good solution is to introduce a soup as a first course to take the edge off the ravenous appetites around the table. Soup, particularly if served with bread, is a filling and cheap start to any meal, as well as a great energy reviver. I have set down here some soups which are very simple to make from scratch.

If you have done some preparation for your main course earlier in the day, you should be able to rustle up these soups in a few minutes when you get back to your apartment in the evening.

French onion soup

This is a particularly filling start to any meal.

Preparation: 5–10 minutes
Cooking: 40 minutes
Serves 4

4 large onions
1 tablespoon butter
1 tablespoon sugar
1 litre (1¾ pints) water

2 beef stock cubes
100g ($3\frac{1}{2}$oz) Emmental cheese, grated
bay leaf
black pepper

Halve the onions and slice them quite thickly, then halve the slices to reduce them to a manageable length (remember you have to be able to eat them from a spoon). Put them in a saucepan with the butter and sugar over a medium heat and fry gently until golden brown. This will take about 5–10 minutes with the occasional stir; you can prepare the rest of the supper in the meantime.

Pour the water on to the onions with the stock cubes and bring to the boil. Add a bay leaf and simmer, covered, for 30–40 minutes, stirring occasionally. Season with pepper and ladle the soup into each bowl. Immediately sprinkle with the grated cheese and serve with bread.

Quick broth

Easy to prepare, this is based on a Chinese recipe. You are unlikely to have soy sauce handy, but a bit of Marmite or a few drops of Worcestershire sauce adds the necessary bite.

Preparation: 10 minutes
Cooking: 5 minutes
Serves 4

225g (8oz) button mushrooms
1 bunch watercress or spring onions
1 litre ($1\frac{3}{4}$ pints) water
2 chicken stock cubes
2 eggs
1 tablespoon soy sauce, few drops Worcestershire sauce or $\frac{1}{2}$ teaspoon Marmite

Slice the mushrooms finely, wash the watercress under the tap and cut the stalks off (or slice the spring onions, including their green stalks). Bring the water and stock cubes to the boil in a saucepan, add the vegetables and simmer for about 5 minutes. Beat the eggs in a mug with a fork then add to the broth with the sauce, whisking lightly. Once the egg has cooked in strands, serve immediately.

Curried lentil soup

Lentils are a good source of protein as well as providing a cheap addition to soups, stews and curries. The orange ones don't need to be soaked in advance and thus are ideal for using on holiday. You can quickly put this on to cook when you get in and leave it unattended for an hour.

Preparation: 5 minutes
Cooking: 1 hour
Serves 4

2 large onions
1 clove garlic
1 tablespoon butter or oil
1 tablespoon mild curry powder
225g (8oz) orange lentils
1¼ litres (2¼ pints) water
2 chicken stock cubes
bay leaf
juice of half lemon
4 thick slices of lemon
black pepper (optional)

Chop the onions and fry them in the butter or oil with the crushed garlic for a few minutes till soft. Stir in the curry powder and lentils and cook for a minute or two to allow the curry powder to absorb some of the fat, then add the water and stock cubes. Bring to the boil with the bay leaf, cover and simmer for 1 hour until the lentils have almost disintegrated.

Add the lemon juice and season if necessary with black pepper. Serve with a thick slice of lemon in each bowl.

17
SUPPER DISHES

BEEF

Beef goulash

Like most beef casseroles, this one needs a couple of hours cooking to make it really tender. But if you get it all ready in the morning, you can put it on to cook the moment you walk in the door. Ask the butcher to cut the meat into cubes for you, to save time.

Morning preparation: 15 minutes
Evening preparation: 5 minutes
Cooking time: 2 hours
Serves 4

1kg (2¼lb) braising beef
2 big onions
2 cloves garlic
3 tablespoons oil
1 level tablespoon paprika
1 tablespoon flour
1 tablespoon tomato purée
200ml (7fl oz) white wine
200ml (7fl oz) beef stock or water
seasoning
bouquet garni
1 red sweet pepper
400g (14oz) tin tomatoes
150ml (¼pint) sour cream or yoghurt

In the morning
Cut the meat into large cubes if the butcher hasn't done this already. Peel and slice the onions, crush the garlic. Heat the oil in a casserole or large saucepan, brown the meat and remove it to a plate. Lower the heat and fry the onions with

the garlic. After a few minutes add the paprika, tomato purée and flour. Cook for a minute, stirring well then mix in the wine and stock or water. Put back the meat with the bouquet garni, cover and leave in the fridge.
In the evening
Bring the casserole to a simmer on top of the stove, then leave to cook on the ring, or transfer to a medium oven (Gas 4/350°F/180°C) for 1½ hours. When this time is up, slice the red pepper and remove the seeds, then add it with the tin of tomatoes to the casserole. Stir well, cook a further 30 minutes and stir in the cream or natural yoghurt before serving.

Beef and red wine casserole

A real *boeuf Bourguignon* uses best rump steak. This is a cheat's, less expensive version, though remember that the cheaper the cut of meat, the longer it will take to cook — the cheapest will need 2 hours. By cooking the potatoes in the casserole with the meat, they soak up the delicious rich sauce.

Morning preparation: 10 minutes
Evening preparation: 15 minutes
Cooking time: 1½–2 hours
Serves 4

1kg (2¼lb) chuck steak (one up from braising)
2 large onions
2 cloves garlic
2-3 tablespoons sunflower oil
pinch dried mixed herbs
seasoning
300ml (½ pint) red wine
300ml (½ pint) water
2 tablespoons tomato purée
700g (1½lb) potatoes

In the morning
Cut the meat into smallish cubes, slice the onions. Put the meat and onions in a dish, pour over the wine and leave, covered, in the fridge for the day.
In the evening
Pour off the wine into a mug or bowl. Heat the oil in a thick-bottomed saucepan (big enough to hold the potatoes as well), and fry the onion with the crushed garlic for a few minutes. Add the meat and brown it over a high heat, then pour on the reserved wine. Simmer until the liquid has reduced a bit then add the tomato purée, water, herbs and

seasoning. Bring to the boil, cover and leave to simmer gently for 1¼ hours.

Peel, and cut the potatoes into chunks if large. Drop them into the casserole and continue cooking a further 15–20 minutes until they are ready.

Chilli con carne

It's better if you prepare and cook this all at once, rather than doing some of it in the morning. If you start it off when you get in, it will be ready to eat in just over an hour, which gives everyone time to shower and broach the duty free bottle you bought on the way out.

Morning preparation: 0
Evening preparation: 15–20 minutes
Cooking time: 1 hour
Serves 6

700g (1½lb) beef mince
2 tablespoons oil
2 large onions
1 clove garlic
2 teaspoons chilli powder
2 × 400g (14oz) tins red kidney beans
400g (14oz) tin tomatoes
little salt

Peel and thinly slice the onions. Heat the oil in a flameproof casserole or large frying pan and fry the onions gently till soft. Add the mince and garlic and stir well until the meat is browned and fairly well broken up. Drain the kidney beans and gently stir them in with the chilli powder and tomatoes. Season with a little salt.

Cover the pan and leave to simmer gently on top of the stove, or in a low oven (Gas 3/325°F/170°C), for 1 hour. Check every 15 minutes or so to make sure it isn't sticking to the bottom. If it seems to be getting a bit dry, add a little hot water.

Tagliatelle alla Bolognese

The old favourite with everyone, but here served with paper-thin egg noodles called *tagliatelle* as a variation. They are a bit easier to eat than *spaghetti*, as well! The meat sauce needs at least 45 minutes to cook, or you'll find it's too watery.

Morning preparation: 5 minutes
Evening preparation: 15 minutes
To cook: 45 minutes
Serves 4

1 large onion
125g (4½oz) mushrooms
1-2 cloves garlic
2 tablespoons oil
700g (1½lb) beef mince
2 level tablespoons flour
400g (14oz) tin tomatoes
2 teaspoons tomato purée
150ml (¼pint) red wine
150ml (¼pint) beef stock
pinch mixed herbs
seasoning
Parmesan cheese
350g (12oz) tagliatelle

In the morning
Peel and chop the onion, rinse the mushrooms and slice them thinly. Leave on a plate, covered, in the fridge.
In the evening
Heat the oil in a saucepan and add the onions with the crushed garlic. Cover and cook gently for 5 minutes. Add the mince, stir well until it is browned and fairly well broken up, then add the mushrooms and cook for a few minutes. Stir in the flour until it absorbs the liquid, then pour in the tomatoes, together with the tomato purée, herbs and seasoning. Stir well, add the wine and stock and bring to the boil. Lower the heat, cover and simmer very gently for 45–60 minutes.

About 15 minutes before eating, bring a large pan of salted water to the boil, add the *tagliatelle* and boil for 12 minutes until tender but not overcooked. (If you are using fresh pasta it will take only 5 minutes.) Pour the sauce over the pasta and have a bowl of grated Parmesan on the table to sprinkle over each portion.

Steak Diane

This really speedy recipe justifies the extra cost if you're in a hurry.

Morning preparation: 0
Evening preparation: 2 minutes
To cook: 5 minutes
Serves 4

4 × 200g (7oz) sirloin steaks
3 tablespoons butter
½ medium onion
4 tablespoons brandy

2 tablespoons Worcestershire sauce
1 tablespoon freshly chopped parsley

Beat the steaks with the side of a heavy tin or similar until they are quite thin. (If you can make the butcher understand, get him to do this for you.) Chop the onion finely. Melt the butter in a large heavy frying pan and cook the onion until golden. Move it to one side of the pan, turn up the heat and add the steaks, quickly sealing them for a couple of minutes on both sides. Add the brandy and stand back as it flames up. When it has died out, add the Worcestershire sauce and parsley. Serve immediately.

Liver Stroganoff

This is an economical version of the classic Beef Stroganoff, which uses fillet steak. Should your budget stretch that far, simply replace the liver with the same quantity of fillet. It is easier to slice liver thinly, especially if your knife is not razor sharp, if it is semi-frozen.

Morning preparation: 0
Evening preparation: 5 minutes
To cook: 20 minutes
Serves 4

700g (1½lb) lambs' or calves' liver
1 medium onion
250g (9oz) mushrooms
2 tablespoons butter
150g (5oz) tub sour cream
4 tablespoons freshly chopped parsley
seasoning

Slice the liver thinly and then cut these slices into matchstick strips. Heat most of the butter in a frying pan and soften the onions, covered with a lid, for 10–15 minutes. Slice the mushrooms, add them and fry gently. Move the vegetables to one side of the pan, add the rest of the butter and, when it is hot, put in the liver strips. Cook them quickly for about 1 minute, turning, then lower the heat and stir in the sour cream and parsley. Season and serve with rice or pasta.

PORK

Pork chops with apple

You can prepare most of this in the morning; but don't slice the apples until just before using them or they turn brown. You need an oven to make this dish.

Morning preparation: 5–10 minutes
Evening preparation: 10 minutes
Cooking time: 45 minutes
Serves 4

4 pork loin chops
2 tablespoons butter
1 large onion
pinch mixed herbs
150ml (1/4 pint) dry white wine
seasoning
500g (1 1/4lb) apples
4 tablespoons fresh white breadcrumbs
3 tablespoons grated Parmesan or hard cheese

In the morning
Trim any surplus fat off the chops. Peel and finely chop the onion. Grease an ovenproof dish with a little butter, arrange the chops on top and sprinkle with the onion and herbs. Season well and pour over the white wine. Leave covered in the fridge.
In the evening
Preheat the oven to hot (Gas 6/400°F/200°C). Peel, core and slice the apples and push the slices down into the marinade covering the chops. Roughly grate a slice or two of bread, or crumble it in your fingers, mix it with the grated cheese and sprinkle over the chops. Dot with butter and cover with a lid or silver foil.

Bake in the hot oven for 45 minutes or until the chops are tender.

Fillet of pork with mushrooms

Pork fillet is not cheap, but if you buy the right cut you can beat it out to make it stretch to feed four people. You need a piece of tenderloin, which is a long sausage shape, which you then cut across the grain into mini escalopes.

Morning preparation: 20 minutes
Evening preparation and cooking: 15 minutes
Serves 4

700g ($1\frac{1}{2}$lb) pork tenderloin fillet
2 tablespoons oil
2 tablespoons lemon juice
black pepper
1 clove garlic
Sauce
150g (5oz) button mushrooms
1 medium onion
2 tablespoons butter
dash white wine
150ml ($\frac{1}{4}$ pint) cream
1 tablespoon flour
seasoning

In the morning
Trim the fat from the pork, cut it across the grain into slices 2.5cm (1in) thick. Put these, 2 at a time, under a piece of wet silver foil or greaseproof paper and beat flat with a rolling pin, heavy tin or back of a wooden spoon. Put the slices into a shallow dish. Pour over the oil and lemon, sprinkle with the black pepper and crushed garlic and leave covered in the fridge. Slice the mushrooms and peel and chop the onion for the sauce, leave covered in the fridge.
In the evening
Melt the butter in a frying pan and fry the onion gently for 5 minutes till soft. Add the mushrooms and fry a few more minutes, then lift these out on to a plate. Lift the pork out of its marinade and fry in the butter, turning once. Transfer to a hot serving dish, cover and keep warm. Add the flour to the pan, make a roux and then add enough wine to make a smooth base. Return the vegetables and add the cream, stir well while reheating but do not allow to boil. Season and pour the sauce over the pork.

Pork casserole

Pork sold under the label 'stewing' or 'for pies' is cheap and tasty, and very good so long as you give it long enough to cook to tenderness. Unsweetened apple juice is a perfectly satisfactory substitute for dry cider. If you can find wild mushrooms in the greengrocers, so much the better, but the ordinary button ones are fine.

Morning preparation: 10 minutes
Evening preparation: 10 minutes
Cooking time: $1\frac{1}{4}$ hours
Serves 4

750g (1¾lb) stewing pork
1 medium onion
2 tablespoons sunflower oil
1 large clove garlic
1 tablespoon plain flour
500ml (¾pint) cider or unsweetened apple juice
large pinch dried thyme
1 bay leaf
seasoning
125g (4½oz) mushrooms

In the morning
Cube the pork and slice the onion, leave covered in the fridge for the day.
In the evening
Fry the onion with the garlic in a frying pan or large saucepan for 5 minutes. Push the onion to one side and add the pork, turning it over a high heat so it browns evenly. Stir in the flour, lower the heat a little and blend in the cider or apple juice. Season well and add the herbs, then cover and leave over a low heat for 1 hour. After this time halve or quarter the mushrooms and add them, cook a further 15 minutes and serve.

Barbecue spare ribs

This is popular with children and others who like to sit gnawing the bones with their elbows on the table, but you need a grill to cook it. Buy the spare ribs used in Chinese cooking, with just a little meat clinging to the bone. Don't worry if you haven't got *all* the different ingredients for the sauce, just improvise – or you might find a bottled barbecue sauce in the supermarket.

Morning preparation: 0
Evening preparation: 5 minutes
Cooking time: 15 minutes
Serves 4

16 spare ribs
4 tablespoons honey or some brown sugar
3 tablespoons soy sauce
3 tablespoons tomato ketchup
few drops Tabasco sauce
1 clove garlic
small teaspoon mustard
pinch paprika
juice of 1 orange
4 tablespoons wine vinegar
2 teaspoons cornflour

Separate the ribs from each other and grill for 10–15 minutes until crispy. Heat all the sauce ingredients together, crushing the garlic, and pour over the ribs when the sauce starts to thicken. Serve with rice.

Chickpea and sausage casserole

To save time and cut down on the steam in your apartment, buy tinned chickpeas which are ready cooked, rather than go through the lengthy soaking and boiling of dried ones.

Morning preparation: 0
Evening preparation: 10 minutes
Cooking time: 30 minutes
Serves 4

1 tablespoon oil
1-2 cloves garlic, crushed
1 medium onion
1 tablespoon tomato purée
large pinch dried mixed herbs
seasoning
400g (14oz) tin tomatoes
2 × 400g (14oz) tins chickpeas
500g (1¼lb) local spicy boiling sausage

Slice the onion and sauté it with the crushed garlic in the oil for a few minutes, in a heavy-bottomed casserole or saucepan. Stir in the tomato purée, then pour in the tomatoes, breaking them up with a fork. Drain the chickpeas and add them, together with the sausage sliced into chunks and the herbs. Season well, cover and simmer for 30 minutes or more. Serve with egg noodles.

Spinach and ham pasta

Pasta dishes always make quick suppers, and this is a cheap way of satisfying hungry appetites. Serve with a big salad, and some cheese and fruit for dessert.

Morning preparation: 5 minutes
Evening preparation: 5 minutes
Cooking: 15 minutes
Serves 4

2 tablespoons oil
2 cloves garlic, crushed
1 medium onion
seasoning
300g (11oz) cooked unsmoked ham
250g (9oz) frozen chopped spinach

325 g (12 oz) pasta spirals, or shapes
small 150 g (5 oz) tub cream

In the morning
Chop the onion and the ham, leave covered in the fridge. Leave the spinach in a bowl to defrost.
In the evening
Put a large pan of water on to boil, and when it is ready, throw in the pasta to cook for 10–12 minutes. If you are using fresh pasta, it will only take 3–5 minutes.

Heat the oil in a saucepan and sauté the onion with the crushed garlic for a few minutes. Add the ham and spinach and cook a further 5 minutes, stirring occasionally. When any excess water from the spinach has cooked away, stir in the cream, season well, reheat and mix into the drained pasta before serving.

Ham and chicory in cheese sauce

If the money is running low and you want a cheap alternative to meat-orientated suppers, try this filling recipe. You need an oven to make this.

Morning preparation: 0
Evening preparation: 10–15 minutes
Cooking: 30 minutes
Serves 4

8 thin slices cooked ham
8 small heads chicory
lemon
600 ml (1 pint) water
1 stock cube
seasoning
1 tablespoon butter
1 packet cheese sauce
100 g ($3\frac{1}{2}$ oz) hard cheese

Trim the chicory and rub it with a cut lemon; this prevents it discolouring. Dissolve the stock cube in a pint of boiling water and simmer the chicory until tender (about 10–15 minutes). Drain. Make the cheese sauce according to the instructions.

Wrap each piece of chicory in a slice of ham, lay in a buttered dish, season and cover with the cheese sauce. Grate the cheese or cut it into thin slices and sprinkle over the dish, then bake in a hot oven for about 15 minutes until brown.

VEAL

Veal and tomato casserole

You can quickly prepare this in the morning, so when you get home all you need to do is bring it to a simmer and leave it to cook while you shower and collapse after a day on the slopes. Ask the butcher to chop the veal into pieces for you – your apartment kitchen is unlikely to contain the right implements for this.

Morning preparation: 10 minutes
Evening preparation: 0
To cook: 2 hours
Serves 4–6

1½kg (3¼lb) veal on the bone (neck, shoulder or knuckle)
2 large onions
2 × 400g (14oz) tins tomatoes
3 tablespoons olive oil
500g (1¼lb) small potatoes (tinned will do)
seasoning
paprika
pinch mixed herbs
150g (5oz) tub sour cream
whole button mushrooms (optional)
large sliced green pepper (optional)

In the morning
Slice the onions and fry them in the oil until golden brown. If you are using fresh rather than tinned potatoes, get someone else to scrub them (peeling is not necessary). Fry the veal until browned all over, sprinkle with the paprika and stir well before pouring in the tomatoes. Season and add the herbs. Leave in a cool place until evening.
In the evening
Bring the casserole to a boil on top of the stove, then lower the heat and leave to simmer for 2 hours, or put it into a moderate oven. After 1½ hours drop in the potatoes; if you can't get small ones, buy normal size and cut into chunks. If you are using tinned potatoes, add them 15–20 minutes before the end of the cooking time.

To pad this out to serve more people, add 100g (3½oz) whole button mushrooms and a large sliced green pepper.

Just before serving, stir in the sour cream. Remember you can sour normal cream by adding a teaspoon of lemon juice.

Saltimbocca

The Italian name for this dish translates as jump-in-the-mouth, referring presumably to its rather special combination of flavours. If asked, the butcher will beat the veal escalopes thin for you. You need some wooden toothpicks or cotton thread to hold the little parcels together.

Morning preparation: 10–15 minutes
To cook: 15 minutes
Serves 4

8 slices veal escalope, depending on size
8 slices Parma ham
fresh sage leaves
2 tablespoons butter
150ml (¼ pint) dry white wine
seasoning

In the morning
Beat each slice of veal until it is very thin, if the butcher has not already done this. Lay a sage leaf and a slice of Parma ham on each piece of veal. Roll up and secure either with a wooden toothpick or by tying with cotton. Leave in the fridge till evening.
To cook
Heat the butter in a frying pan and brown the veal rolls for a few minutes, turning quickly. Add the white wine and seasoning and simmer for a further 5–10 minutes, then remove the sticks or cut the thread and serve.

Orange-glazed veal chops

Delicious and very quick to prepare and cook, this is a cheaper way of eating veal than blowing your budget with restaurant prices. Loin chops are less expensive than escalopes, though neither are exactly cheap.

Morning preparation: 0
Evening preparation: 3 minutes
Cooking time: 10 minutes
Serves 6

6 veal escalopes or loin chops
1 onion
2 tablespoons butter
1 big clove garlic
pinch dried thyme
1 wineglass orange juice
2-3 tablespoons cream
seasoning

Chop the onion finely. Sauté the onion and the crushed garlic in the butter, in a frying pan over quite a high heat. After a few minutes add the veal chops or escalopes and fry for 2 minutes or so before turning over and browning the other side too. Pile the veal up on one side of the pan and pour the orange juice in. Let it reduce in quantity a little before stirring in the cream. Season well, and when it has reached a syrupy consistency, serve the veal with the sauce poured over.

CHICKEN

Chicken in red wine
(*coq au vin*)

This classic French casserole is always popular. Don't skimp on the wine or you won't get the same rich sauce.

Morning preparation: 5–10 minutes
Evening preparation: 10–15 minutes
Cooking time: 1 hour
Serves 4

1½kg (3¼lb) chicken or 4 chicken quarters
125g (4½oz) streaky bacon
125g (4½oz) button onions or 1½ medium ones
2 tablespoons butter
½ bottle Burgundy or soft red wine
3 tablespoons brandy
2 cloves garlic
bouquet garni
seasoning

In the morning
Joint the chicken if you bought a whole one. Cut the rind off the bacon and dice it. If you are using a whole onion, peel it, cut into quarters, then cut these in half across. Leave covered in the fridge till evening.
In the evening
Brown the chicken joints slowly in the butter in a flameproof casserole or large saucepan, then remove them to a plate. Add the onions and bacon, brown a little then replace the chicken. Pour on the brandy and set it alight (keep a lid handy in case it flames up too high). This stage gives the dish its special flavour. Add the wine, bring to the boil and set this alight as well. Crush the garlic and add it with the bouquet garni and seasoning, cover and simmer for 1 hour.

Braised chicken in lemon sauce

The taste of lemons makes this a really special meal. If you can't find sour cream, add a teaspoon or two of lemon juice to ordinary cream.

Morning preparation: 5–10 minutes
Evening preparation: 5–10 minutes
Cooking time: 1 hour
Serves 4

1½kg (3¼lb) chicken or 4 chicken quarters
bunch parsley
4 rashers streaky bacon
seasoning
ground nutmeg
juice of ½ lemon
150ml (¼ pint) water

Sauce
2 tablespoons butter
1 rounded tablespoon flour
juice of ½ lemon
300ml (½ pint) milk
150ml (¼ pint) sour cream

In the morning
Joint the chicken or cut the quarters into joints. Grease the casserole or saucepan with butter, line it with bacon and place the chicken pieces on top, with the parsley strewn over them, unchopped but washed. Season well and add a pinch of ground nutmeg. Squeeze the lemon juice into a mug, pick out the pips, then add it with about 150ml (¼ pint) water to the dish. Cover and leave in the fridge.
In the evening
Simmer chicken very gently on top of the stove for 45–60 minutes until it is tender, checking occasionally to see if you need to add any more (hot) water.

About 10 minutes before the end of cooking time make the sauce. Make a roux by melting the butter in a saucepan and stirring in the flour, then adding the milk and lemon juice, stirring well to avoid lumps forming. When it is quite smooth, blend in the cream, heat through but don't boil. Lift out the chicken and pour the sauce over.

Paprika chicken

No morning preparation here, so you can sleep in after a night on the town. It's quick to prepare and excellent served with rice or noodles. If you can't get sour cream, add a squeeze of lemon juice to ordinary cream about 10 minutes before using.

Morning preparation: 0
Evening preparation: 5–10 minutes
Cooking time: 30 minutes
Serves 4

4 chicken breasts
2 tablespoons flour
seasoning
2 tablespoons oil
1 large onion
2 heaped teaspoons paprika
150ml (¼ pint) water or chicken stock
3 tomatoes
1 red or green sweet pepper
150ml (¼ pint) sour cream

Coat the chicken breasts in seasoned flour. Heat the oil in a frying pan and brown the sliced onion. Add the chicken and fry gently. Stir in the paprika, and gradually add the water, stirring well.

Cover and simmer for 10 minutes while you slice the tomatoes and deseed and slice the sweet pepper. Add these, return to the boil and simmer for a further 20 minutes. Stir in the cream, heat through and serve.

Chicken in white wine

Chicken casseroles cooked on top of the stove are ideal easy supper dishes. This one has the vegetables cooked in with it, so only one ring is used to produce the whole meal.

Morning preparation: 5–10 minutes
Evening preparation: 15 minutes
Cooking time: 45 minutes
Serves 4

1½kg (3¼lb) chicken or 4 quarters
4 carrots
75g (3oz) mushrooms
1 medium onion
8 small potatoes
2 tablespoons flour
seasoning
2 tablespoons oil or butter
pinch mixed herbs
bouquet garni
½ bottle dry white wine

In the morning
Quarter the chicken if you have bought a whole one. Slice the carrots, peel and chop the onion, and chop the mushrooms. Cover and leave in the fridge.
In the evening
Coat the chicken in seasoned flour. Heat the oil or butter and

gently fry the onion, turn up the heat and brown the chicken pieces. Add the mushrooms, cook a minute or two then stir in the white wine. Sprinkle with the herbs, add the bouquet garni, then cover and bring to the boil.

Simmer gently for 25 minutes. Peel and halve the potatoes and drop them in after this time with the carrots. (Add a little hot water or chicken stock if the liquid is getting very low.) Return to the boil and cook a further 20 minutes.

You might like to serve bread with this dish to mop up the juices.

Chicken with peaches

This is an unusual dish that requires minimum preparation and tastes delicious – a kind of sweet and sour combination. You need an oven for this dish.

Morning preparation: 1 minute
Evening preparation: 5 minutes
Cooking time: 1 hour
Serves 4

1½kg (3¼lb) chicken or 4 quarters
2 tablespoons butter
400g (14oz) tin sliced peaches
Sauce
1 tablespoon honey
pinch dried oregano
1 tablespoon Worcestershire sauce
2 tablespoons French mustard
5 tablespoons white wine vinegar
dash Tabasco sauce

In the morning
Leave the butter out of the fridge when you go out in the morning, so it is quite soft by the evening.
In the evening
Joint the chicken if you have bought a whole one. Rub the pieces all over with the butter and place them in a casserole. Mix together all the sauce ingredients and pour them over the chicken. Cover and cook in a hot oven (Gas 6/400°F/200°C) for 35–45 minutes.

Add the tin of peaches, with juice, to the casserole. Stir the sauce and cook for a further 15 minutes, covered.

One pot casserole

This is best made with cheap cuts of lamb (get the butcher to cut middle neck pieces into chunks), but is equally successful with chicken, where the cooking time is less. Incredibly quick to prepare.

Morning preparation: 0
Evening preparation: 5–10 minutes
Cooking: 1–1½ hours (45–60 minutes for chicken)
Serves 4

2 tablespoons oil
2 cloves garlic, crushed
1.5kg (3½lb) lamb or chicken pieces on the bone
2 × 400g (14oz) tins chopped tomatoes
1 large onion
splash red wine
pinch dried mixed herbs
400g (14oz) tin haricot or cannellini beans
400g (14oz) tin potatoes

Slice the onion and quickly fry it in the hot oil with the crushed garlic, in a big saucepan over a high heat. Add the meat and brown it on all sides quickly, removing each piece as it is done. Pour on the wine, stir well, add the tomatoes and herbs and return the meat to the pan. Bring to a simmer, cover, and cook on top of the stove or in a low oven for 1½ hours (45–60 minutes if you're using chicken pieces).

About 10 minutes before the end, stir in the tinned beans and reheat gently on top of the stove.

FISH

Stuffed trout in white wine

This is very simple and quite delicious. You need an oven and some silver foil. You can use frozen trout, but if buying fresh, ask the supplier to gut the fish for you.

Morning preparation: 0
Evening preparation: 5 minutes
Cooking time: 15–20 minutes
Serves 4

4 trout
1 lemon
1 head fennel or 1 medium onion

1-2 glasses white wine
3 tablespoons butter
bay leaves
seasoning

Wash the trout and pat dry. Chop the onion or fennel head very finely, discarding the tough central core and root of the fennel. Rub the inside of 4 pieces of silver foil, large enough to wrap each fish in, with the butter. Fill the cavities of each fish with the chopped onion or fennel, a slice or two of lemon, a bay leaf and some seasoning. Lay each fish on the foil and bring the sides up to form an envelope. Splash in a little dry white wine, crimp the edges together to seal and put each parcel on a baking tray. Cook in an oven preheated to Gas 6/400°F/200°C for 15–20 minutes.

Seafood pilaff

Fresh seafood is not available up in the mountains, but this pilaff uses tinned shellfish to create a simple light supper.

Morning preparation: 0
Evening preparation: 10 minutes
Cooking time: 15–20 minutes
Serves 4

2 tablespoons butter
½ medium onion
1 clove garlic, crushed
2 mugs water
1 chicken stock cube
1 heaped mug white rice
200g (7oz) tin crab meat
200g (7oz) packet frozen prawns
170g (6oz) tin pimentos
seasoning

Chop the onion. Melt half the butter in a saucepan and fry the onion with the crushed garlic for a few minutes, then add the rice, stir well and pour on the water with the stock cube. Bring to the boil, stir until the stock cube has dissolved then cover and leave to cook over a low heat. After 15–20 minutes the rice should have absorbed the stock, check just before to make sure it isn't sticking, and add a little more boiling water if necessary.

Drain and slice the pimentos, and fry them with the crab meat and defrosted prawns in the rest of the butter. Mix into the rice with a fork, season well and serve with a big salad.

Shellfish pasta sauce

A storecupboard dish that relies on the supermarket freezer and the delicatessen shelves, this is quick and easy to prepare.

Morning preparation: 0
Evening preparation: 10 minutes
Cooking time: 30 minutes
Serves 4

350g (12oz) pasta shells or spirals
175g (6oz) frozen prawns
2 small tins smoked oysters or mussels
4 tinned artichoke bases
1 medium onion
1 clove garlic
1 tablespoon oil
400g (14oz) tin tomatoes
dash dry white wine
pinch dried mixed herbs
seasoning

Defrost the prawns earlier in the day. Chop the onion and sauté it in the oil with the crushed garlic in a saucepan. Add the tomatoes, wine, herbs and seasoning and simmer, covered for 20 minutes. Slice the artichoke bases and add them with the drained oysters or mussels and the defrosted prawns. Put the pasta on to cook in a large pan of boiling salted water. Simmer the sauce a further 5–10 minutes, drain the pasta and serve it up with the sauce poured over.

Storecupboard tuna bake

Here's a recipe for when you've just arrived, or haven't had time to get to the shops. You need an oven to make this dish.

Morning preparation: 0
Evening preparation: 5 minutes
Cooking: 20 minutes + 15 minutes for the pasta
Serves 6

325g (12oz) dried green tagliatelli
2 × 200g (7oz) tins tuna
400g (14oz) can condensed mushroom soup
seasoning
125g (4oz) Emmental cheese
1 packet potato crisps or similar

Bring a large pan of salted water to the boil and cook the

tagliatelli for 10–12 minutes. Drain the tuna fish, flake it and mix with the condensed soup. Season well and mix into the cooked, drained *tagliatelli*, then transfer the whole lot to a shallow greased oven dish. Grate the cheese or slice it finely, and cover the dish with it. Crumble the crisps over the top and bake in a hot oven for 15–20 minutes until golden brown.

Serve with a plain green salad.

18

SALADS

If your kitchen is a bit cramped, and particularly if you only have two rings on which to cook, it is a good idea to make a salad to accompany the main course. Alternatively, if you are serving a big bowl of filling soup, a hefty salad with bread may be all you need to follow. So long as you don't put any dressing on, salads can be made in advance and kept in the fridge till your evening meal.

It is quicker, cheaper and simpler to buy a bottle or two of ready-made French dressing, unless you will be eating salad every day, in which case it is more economical to buy the oil and vinegar and make your own. Ready-made mayonnaise is also a good buy.

Red cabbage salad

Preparation: 5–10 minutes
Cooking: 5 minutes
Serves 6

½ large or 1 small red cabbage
3 sticks celery
2 crisp apples
small packet walnuts
small tub (150g; 5oz) sour cream
seasoning
2 tablespoons French dressing

Remove the outer leaves from the cabbage and quarter it. Cut out the core, and slice the cabbage thinly. Throw it into a pan of boiling water and simmer for a minute to soften very slightly, then drain and run under cold water. Core and chop the apple, slice the celery, chop the walnuts and mix in with the salad. Season well and stir in the sour cream, mixed with a tablespoon or two of French dressing.

Cooked vegetable salad (Russian salad)

Tinned Russian salad is rather nasty— but if you use some tinned vegetables mixed with a couple of fresh ones for 'bite' the result is much more appetising.

Preparation: 10–15 minutes
Cooking: 5 minutes
Serves 6

400g (14oz) tin new potatoes
1 small cauliflower
1 small packet frozen peas
1 small packet frozen French beans
3 medium carrots
4 sticks celery
4 tablespoons French dressing
1 cup mayonnaise
2 tablespoons natural yoghurt
seasoning
1 tablespoon fresh chopped parsley

Strain and slice the potatoes. Cut the cauliflower into little florets; cook the beans and peas for the minimum time on the packet. Dice the celery and carrots and boil them with the cauliflower for 2 minutes only in slightly salted water (you can use the same water as you cooked the frozen vegetables in). Mix all the vegetables together while still warm and spoon the French dressing over. Cool and then stir the yoghurt and mayonnaise together, season well and mix into the salad. Sprinkle with the parsley and serve with hot frankfurters.

Three bean salad

You can make this from the storecupboard, and you will find it is fairly filling. The onion does add a bit of sharpness, which is a necessary contrast, so don't omit it.

Preparation: 5 minutes
Cooking: 0
Serves 4–6

400g (14oz) tin white haricot beans or cannellini
400g (14oz) tin red kidney beans

400g (14oz) chickpeas
1 medium onion
4-5 tablespoons French dressing
1 teaspoon French mustard
2 tablespoons fresh chopped parsley
seasoning

Drain the beans well and put them in a bowl. Slice the onion finely and add with the chopped parsley and seasoning to give a more pungent flavour. Mix the mustard with the French dressing and pour over the salad.

Salad Niçoise

Here is another filling salad if you're planning a cold supper with perhaps a soup to start.

Morning cooking: 10 minutes
Evening preparation: 10 minutes
Serves 4

2 eggs
55g (2oz) tin anchovies
little milk
200g (7oz) tin tuna
1 tablespoon mayonnaise (optional)
2 tomatoes
1 green pepper
1 good sized lettuce
2 tablespoons black olives (preferably stoned)
4-5 tablespoons French dressing

In the morning
Hard boil the eggs and shell them while still warm. Open the anchovies, drain them and leave in a small bowl with a little milk, to soak out some of the saltiness.
In the evening
Drain the tuna and mix it with a little mayonnaise if you wish. Quarter the eggs and tomatoes. Chop the green pepper. Remove the outer leaves from the lettuce, wash it and tear the leaves into small pieces. Use them to line a shallow dish and then scatter the green pepper over the lettuce. Arrange the tuna in the centre, and the tomato and egg quarters all around the edge. Split the anchovies lengthways and arrange them lattice fashion across the salad, add the olives and pour the French dressing over.

Serve with crusty bread.

Fennel salad

Fennel is a good vegetable to buy since it stays fresh for some time out of a fridge, is easy to prepare and gives a very definite taste to anything you mix it with. Try it on its own too, just served with a lemon dressing. This would make an excellent starter with a little smoked local ham.

Morning preparation: 10 minutes
Cooking: 5 minutes
Serves 4

2 medium fennel bulbs
4-6 tablespoons olive oil
½ lemon
seasoning

Trim the fennel bulbs, halve them and cut out the tough central core. Slice them finely. Bring a pan of water to the boil and drop in the fennel for a minute, then drain and run under cold water.

Transfer the slices into a bowl, mix the olive oil with the juice of half a lemon and the seasoning and leave all day to absorb the flavours, before serving as above.

Green salads

Going abroad is the perfect chance to enjoy all the exciting types of lettuce available, which are only just beginning to appear in shops in England. Even the 'basic' everyday lettuce in most of the countries covered here is crisp and tastier than our floppy ones, and you will be surprised how many interesting salad ingredients you will find in Alpine ski resorts, even in the depths of winter.

Radicchio is a purple cabbage-type lettuce with tightly wrapped leaves and a strong, quite bitter taste. A small head will do two or more salads if mixed with other lettuces.

Curly endive or *frisé* lettuce is easily recognisable by its frilly frond-like leaves. The centre is pale green, almost yellow, and the best part. Avoid the outer leaves which can be very bitter.

Reddish-tinged green lettuces like *feuille de chêne* (oakleaf), *lollo rosso* or *quattro stagioni* are popular. They are tastier than a plain lettuce, though not bitter, and are excellent served plain with a good French dressing.

Lamb's lettuce (*mâche*) has small tongue-shaped leaves about the size of your thumb and is usually a good buy when you can find it. It has a delicate flavour and lovely velvety texture.

Batavia is a crisp plain lettuce with light green leaves, which provides a good basic salad to mix with the stronger-tasting varieties like *frisé* or *radicchio*.

19

PARTY-TIME COCKTAILS

Apart from trying out the local wines, beers and spirits, there will be times in your apartment when you want to concoct a few cocktails or brews yourself, perhaps on your last night, or if you make some friends and decide to ask them round for a small party one evening. The recipes below take into account that not only will you have the regional spirits to experiment with, but also a supply of duty free whisky, gin, vodka and so on that you will have bought on your journey out. Few people see après-ski and drinking alchol as two separate activities – but remember that strenuous exertion on the slopes the next day tends not to help a hangover! I have therefore included a couple of suggestions for the morning-after-the-night-before!

Mulled wine
(*Glühwein*)

This is best known in Switzerland and Austria, but also served in many restaurants and cafés in Italy and France. You can buy the spices ready mixed in little 'teabags' on a string, but if you can't find these, here are the quantities. It is of course cheaper to make your own if you already have the spices. Makes about 12 glasses.

2 bottles full-bodied red wine
1 wine glass brandy
2 wine glasses orange juice
2 cinnamon sticks
1 teaspoon cloves
½ wine glass brown sugar

Heat all the ingredients together in a saucepan until the liquid almost reaches simmering point. Keep it that way for 15 minutes (don't allow it to boil or you'll kill off the alcohol – and the party!). Strain into mugs, or, if you're using glasses, put a teaspoon in each one first, to prevent their cracking while you pour.

Sangria

Although this is originally a Spanish drink, it is not uncommon to find it in the more anglicised resorts, especially at parties laid on by tour companies to welcome new arrivals. Beware – it slips down as easily as a soft drink, which it definitely is *not*. Makes about 15 glasses.

2 bottles soft red wine
2 large bottles soda water or fizzy mineral water or 1 bottle soda and ½ bottle of clear lemonade
sliced oranges, lemons, peaches

Thirty minutes before serving, pour the wine over the fruit in large jugs or similar clean containers. Add some ice. Just before pouring mix in the chilled soda water (and lemonade if you are using it) and stir well.

Brandy wine cup

Makes about 20 glasses.

3 bottles dry white wine, chilled
quarter bottle Cognac or other grape brandy
3 liqueur glasses Benedictine (optional)
225g (8oz) tin pineapple chunks
600ml (1 pint) clear lemonade

Soak the pineapple pieces in the brandy at the bottom of a large jug or bowl for about half an hour. Add the chilled wine, liqueur and some ice. Pour in the lemonade with some more ice, just before serving.

Classic Martini

You can make this in a tumbler rather than a cocktail shaker, which you are unlikely to have to hand. The amount of vermouth you add depends on how 'dry' you like your martinis.

3 measures gin
½ measure dry vermouth
twist lemon peel or an olive

Put some ice cubes into a mixing glass and pour on the gin and vermouth. Stir well, pour into a small glass before the ice has started to melt, and keeping the ice cube in the mixing glass. Decorate with the lemon or olive (or a pearl onion, which makes it a Gibson Martini).

Negroni

You will find this served in bars in Italy, where they are somewhat liberal with the measures. A powerful drink!

1 measure Campari
1 measure gin
1 measure Martini Rosso
soda water
slices orange

Put some ice cubes into a glass, pour on the Campari, gin and Martini and stir well. Top up with soda water, decorate with a slice of orange.

Different combinations of straight spirits and mixers which are very good are whisky or gin and fresh orange juice, rum (preferably light brown variety) and tonic water, and vermouth and tonic.

THE MORNING AFTER

For those who feel a little jaded and aren't going out on the slopes first thing, a mid-morning Bloody Mary or Bullshot make great pick me ups. For more serious after effects, try a Prairie Oyster.

Bloody Mary

A true version of this must have all the extras; the vodka and tomato juice served lukewarm in British pubs is no comparison.

1 measure vodka
3 measures tomato juice
dash Worcestershire sauce
dash Tabasco sauce
¼ lemon
small pinch celery salt (ordinary salt will do on holiday)

Half fill a tumbler with ice, pour on the sauces, a big squeeze of lemon juice and add the celery salt. Stir well, pour on the vodka and tomato juice and stir again. Serve with a slice of lemon.

Bullshot

You must dilute concentrated consommé before using it in this recipe. If using ready-to-drink consommé, make sure you buy the kind that stays liquid while cold, rather than becoming jellified, or you'll have unattractive lumps of consommé floating around in your drink!

1 measure vodka
3 measures tinned beef consommé
dash Worcestershire sauce
¼ lemon
small pinch celery salt (or ordinary salt)
black pepper
Garnish
Thin sticks of celery

Half fill a tumbler with ice. Add the Worcestershire sauce, a big squeeze of lemon juice, the celery salt and a little ground black pepper, and stir. Pour on the consommé and vodka and stir well. Serve with a thin stick of celery.

Prairie Oyster

This is a kill or cure one. Only the brave or the desperate can face it.

1 egg yolk
cayenne pepper
dash Worcestershire sauce
dash Tabasco sauce
1 teaspoon wine vinegar
1 measure brandy

Mix all the ingredients except the egg yolk in a tumbler. Carefully add the egg yolk, keeping it whole, and swirl it around the glass. Then drink the whole lot in one gulp. You can also make this omitting the brandy.

For those who can brave it, a measure of Fernet Branca, an evil-smelling Italian bitters, swallowed all in one go, is in fact a great stomach settler, whether you're suffering from the after effects of too much food *or* drink.

20

USEFUL PHRASES

Do you speak English?	F:	*Parlez-vous anglais?*
	G:	*Sprechen Sie Englisch?*
	I:	*Parli inglese?*
I'm sorry, I don't speak French/German/Italian	F:	*Je regrette, je ne parle pas francais.*
	G:	*Es tut mir leid aber ich spreche kein Deutsch.*
	I:	*Mi dispiace, non parlo italiano.*
Excuse me . . .	F:	*Excusez-moi . . .*
	G:	*Entschuldigen Sie . . .*
	I:	*Mi scusi . . .*
Please*	F:	*S'il vous plaît*
	G:	*Bitte*
	I:	*Per favore*
Thank you*	F:	*Merci*
	G:	*Danke*
	I:	*Grazie*

*In French and German, if you are offered more food, drink, etc., you should say thank you if you mean no and please for yes.

Do you have a carrier bag?	F: *Avez-vous un sac?* G: *Haben Sie eine Tüte?* I: *Avete una bolsa?*
How much is it?	F: *Combien est-il?* G: *Wieviel kostet das?* I: *Quanto costa?*
That is too expensive, is there something cheaper?	F: *C'est trop cher, est-ce qu'il y a quelque chose de plus bon marché?* G: *Das ist zu teuer, gibt es etwas billigeres?* I: *E troppo caro, c'è qualcosa di meno caro?*
What time do you close?	F: *A quelle heure fermez-vous?* G: *Um wieviel Uhr schliessen Sie?* I: *A che ora chiudete?*
Are you open on ...?	F: *Etes vous ouvert le ...?* G: *Sind Sie am ... offen?* I: *Siete aperti il ...?*
Monday	F: *lundi* G: *Montag* I: *lunedi*
Tuesday	F: *mardi* G: *Dienstag* I: *martedi*
Wednesday	F: *mercredi* G: *Mittwoch* I: *mercoledi*
Thursday	F: *jeudi* G: *Donnerstag* I: *giovedi*
Friday	F: *vendredi*

	G: *Freitag* I: *venerdi*
Saturday	F: *samedi* G: *Samstag/Sonnabend* I: *sabato*
Sunday	F: *dimanche* G: *Sonntag* I: *domenica*
Where is ...?	F: *Où est ...?* G: *Wo ist ...?* I: *Dove è ...?*
The supermarket	F: *le supermarché* G: *der Supermarkt* I: *il supermercato*
The butcher	F: *la boucherie* G: *die Fleischerei/die Metzgerei* I: *la macelleria*
The baker	F: *la boulangerie* G: *die Bäckerei* I: *la panetteria*
The wine shop	F: *le marchand du vin* G: *die Wein und Spirituosenhandlung* I: *la enoteca*
The bank	F: *la banque* G: *die Bank* I: *la banca*
The chemist	F: *la pharmacie* G: *die Apotheke* I: *la farmacia*
I have no change.	F: *Je n'ai pas de monnaie.* G: *Ich habe kein Kleingeld.* I: *Non ho il resto.*

Can I exchange money here?	F: *Puis-je changer de l'argent ici?* G: *Kann ich hier Geld wechseln?* I: *Posso cambiare dei soldi qui?*
Is this local/from the region?	F: *Est-ce qu'il est local/de la région?* G: *Stammt das von hierher?* I: *È tipica della regione?*
Is there a deposit on the bottle?	F: *Est-ce qu'il y a un dépôt sur la bouteille?* G: *Ist sie mit Flaschenpfand zurückzugeben?* I: *Vuoto a rendere?*
What do you recommend?	F: *Que me recommandez-vous?* G: *Was empfehlen Sie mir?* I: *Cosa consiglia?*
Does it contain sugar/salt/additives?	F: *Est-ce que cela contient du sucre/du sel/des additives?* G: *Enthält das Zucker/Salz/Zusätze?* I: *Contiene zucchero/sale/additivi?*
Sparkling mineral water	F: *eau minérale gazeuse* G: *Mineralwasser mit Gas* I: *acqua minerale con gaz*
Still	F: *naturelle* G: *natur* I: *sin gaz*
That is too big/small/little.	F: *C'est trop grand/petit/peu.*

	G: *Das ist zu gross/klein/ wenig.* I: *È troppo grande/piccolo.*
How long does it take to cook?	F: *Ça prend combien de temps à cuire?* G: *Wie lange dauert es zu kochen?* I: *Quanto tempo ci vuole per cucinare?*
How do you cook it?	F: *Comment le cuit-on?* G: *Wie kocht man das?* I: *Come lo cucini?*
grilled/roasted/baked/boiled	F: *grillé/rôti/cuit au four/bouilli* G: *gegrillt/gebraten/ gebacken/gekocht* I: *ai ferri/arrostito/al forno/lesso*
raw	F: *cru* G: *roh* I: *crudo*
cooked	F: *cuit* G: *gekocht* I: *cotto*
takeaway	F: *à emporter* G: *zu mitnehmen* I: *da portare via*
speciality of the house/ region	F: *spécialité de la maison/ région* G: *Spezialität des Hauses/ der Gegend* I: *specialità della casa/ della regione*
I can't eat food containing ...	F: *je ne peux pas manger des plats avec ...*

	G: *Ich kann keine Speise mit ... essen*
	I: *Non posso mangiare cibo che contiene ...*
I like/I don't like	F: *J'aime/je n'aime pas*
	G: *Ich mag/ich mag nicht*
	I: *Mi piace/non mi piace*
Can you wrap it please?	F: *Pouvez-vous me l'envelopper?*
	G: *Könnten Sie es bitte einwickeln?*
	I: *Me lo può incartare per favore?*
I would like ...	F: *Je voudrais ...*
	G: *Ich möchte ...*
	I: *Vorrei ...*

Weights and Measures

The following tables are approximate and simplified for easy conversion.

SOLID		LIQUID	
Ounces	*Grams*	*British Imperial*	*Metric*
½	15	1 fl oz	25 ml
1	25	2½ fl oz	75 ml
2	50	5 fl oz (¼ pt)	150 ml
2½	60		
3	75	½ pt	300 ml
3½	100	1 pt	600 ml
4	125	1¼ pt	750 ml
5	150	1¾ pt	1 litre
6	175		
7	200	*American*	*Metric*
8	225	1 fl oz	30 ml
9	250	2 fl oz	60 ml
10	280	3 fl oz	90 ml
11	300	4 fl oz	120 ml
12	350	5 fl oz	150 ml
1 lb	450		
2¼ lb	1 kg	½ pt	¼ litre
3 lb	1½ kg	1 pt	½ litre
		1½ pts	¾ litre
		2 pts	1 litre

OVEN TEMPERATURES

	Celsius	Gas	Fahrenheit
Very cool	130°	½	250°
	140°	1	275°
Cool	150°	2	300°
Warm	170°	3	325°
Moderate	180°	4	350°
Fairly hot	190°	5	375°
	200°	6	400°
Hot	220°	7	425°
Very hot	230°	8	450°
	240°	9	475°
	250°	10	500°

MEASUREMENTS

0.4in	1cm
0.8in	2cm
1.2in	3cm
1.6in	4cm
2in	5cm
2.4in	6cm
2.8in	7cm
3in	8cm
3.5in	9cm

Index